The Completely
Unofficial *Glee*

The Completely Unofficial *Glee*

S A R A H O L I V E R

JOHN BLAKE

Published by John Blake Publishing Ltd,
3 Bramber Court, 2 Bramber Road,
London W14 9PB, England

www.johnblakepublishing.co.uk

First published in paperback in 2010

ISBN: 978 1 84358 193 2

British Library Cataloguing-in-Publication Data:

A catalogue record for this book is available from the British Library.

Design by www.envydesign.co.uk

Printed in Great Britain by CPI Bookmarque, Croydon, CR0 4TD

3 5 7 9 10 8 6 4 2

Papers used by John Blake Publishing are natural, recyclable products
made from wood grown in sustainable forests. The manufacturing processes
conform to the environmental regulations of the country of origin.

All photographs have been supplied courtesy of WENN Images.

Dedicated with love to my grandparents,
Harry, Elsie, Norman and Dot

INTRODUCTION

The Completely Unofficial Glee *A–Z* is jam-packed with everything you need to know about *Glee*. No other book goes into so much detail, or tells all the set secrets and what really happened during the kissing scenes. Sarah Oliver is a celebrity journalist who knows more about *Glee* than any other journalist on the planet. She has worked with *Glee* fans across the world to produce the most up-to-date guide to everyone's favourite TV series.

You can read this book from start to finish, or dip in and out of it, as you prefer.

A is for...

'Acafellas' – Season 1, Episode 3

The third episode of *Glee* was called 'Acafellas'. This episode premiered in the USA on 16 September 2009 and first hit the UK screens on 18 January 2010.

In this episode, Will tells his parents that Terri is expecting a baby. As Terri shows Will's mum her craft room, which will become the newborn's room, Will has a heart-to-heart with his dad and admits to him that he has mixed feelings about becoming a father himself.

At school, Will is upset when Rachel casts doubt on his ability to choreograph. She says that New Directions needs the help of Dakota Stanley, who also coaches Vocal Adrenaline. Rachel doesn't realise that she is

JOSH GROBAN WAS A
GUEST STAR IN THE
EPISODE 'ACAFELLAS'.

playing into the hands of Quinn – Brittany and Santana have made her think like this in an attempt to bring down the Glee club.

Will goes for a bite to eat and ends up talking to Sandy, Ken, the school's wood shop teacher Henri and Howard, a colleague of Terri's from Sheets-N-Things. Henri has only just returned to school after accidentally cutting off his thumbs and Howard has brought him a 'welcome back' cake. The men all sing 'For He's a Jolly Good Fellow' to cheer Henri up, but half way through Will realises that they sound really, really good. He thinks they should form an all-male a cappella group.

The guys head to Will's place to practise, minus Sandy who they deem too creepy. After coming up with various names including 'Testostertones' and 'Crescendudes', they settle for Howard's suggestion of 'Acafellas'. Once they've gone, Terri drags Will off to bed. He thinks she finds him sexier now that he's a member of the group but, in reality, she's just trying to get pregnant.

Rachel is starting to feel guilty for knocking Will's choreography skills and tries to get him back onside by giving him her freshly baked cookies. Will isn't interested as he's enjoying being in the Acafellas so much that he doesn't feel that he needs New Directions anymore.

Will and the rest of the Acafellas perform at a local sports bar and prove to be a big hit. Both Terri and Emma swoon over Will and Terri realises that she'll have to keep an eye on the school guidance counsellor. Despite the success of their first performance, Henri and Howard quit. Will finds great replacements in Finn and Noah 'Puck', although Sandy insists that he joins the group because he has arranged for Josh Groban to be at their second performance.

Josh Groban is an American singer-songwriter who has sold almost 20 million albums worldwide. His albums have topped the charts in the USA, Canada and Poland. They have been in the Top Ten in Australia, France, the Netherlands and Sweden. To date he hasn't cracked the UK but it's only a matter of time.

Because Will is so busy with the Acafellas, the Glee club decide to go ahead and hire Dakota Stanley. They need to raise some cash first and so they do a spot of car washing. The Cheerios enjoy tricking Mercedes into thinking that Kurt wants to date her and she is left feeling extremely hurt and confused when he knocks her back. In anger, she throws a rock through his car's windscreen because she thinks he's in love with Rachel.

Their first rehearsal with Dakota goes disastrously wrong when the choreographer insults everyone apart from the cheerleaders. Quinn thinks his harsh words will make some members quit, but Rachel ignores Dakota and remains positive, telling the other members of the Glee club that it is their differences that make them so special. She fires Dakota on the spot.

The Acafellas perform their version of 'I Wanna Sex You Up' at the PTA meeting and it raises a few eyebrows but everyone is impressed with the dancing and singing skills on offer. Josh Groban compliments them but says he only came to the performance to stop Sandy from stalking him.

Will realises that his heart is in teaching, not performing on stage and he decides that he must go back to New Directions and give them all the help he can so they can make Nationals.

Mercedes apologises to Kurt for the rock-throwing incident and he confesses to her that he is gay. They both decide just to be friends. Meanwhile, Sue is furious that New Directions are even closer after her Dakota plan backfired. She needs to come up with a new scheme sharpish if she wants to bring them down.

This episode had many Broadway legends as guest stars. John Lloyd played the wood shop teacher Henri St. Pierre and Will's parents were played by Victor Garber and Debra Monk. The cast performed covers of 'For He's a Jolly Good Fellow', 'This Is How We Do It' by Montell Jordan, 'Poison' by Bell Biv DeVoe, 'Mercy' by Duffy, 'Bust Your Windows' by Jazmine Sullivan, 'La Camisa Negra' by Juanes and 'I Wanna Sex You Up' by Color Me Badd. The *Glee* cast's versions of 'Mercy' and 'Bust Your Windows' were released for download and 'Bust Your Windows' was also included on the first *Glee* album, *Glee: The Music, Volume 1*.

Amber Riley

One of the most talented members of the *Glee* cast is Amber Riley and she is so happy to be playing diva-ish Mercedes Jones in the hit series.

Amber has always been a singer and, even as a child, she loved performing. She started singing when she was

INSIDER GOSSIP

The *Glee* creators, Ryan Murphy, Ian Brennan and Brad Falchuk, didn't think that Josh Groban would be interested in starring in an episode of the series because they thought he was out of their league. They were really surprised when he said he'd love to be part of it.

Josh admits: 'When I first got the script I could just tell they were playing it a little safe, they didn't know how far I would go with it and I just said, "This is supposed to be fun and funny" and I was like, that's hilarious, could I be creepier? You know, make it something you know that I can actually have fun with, okay?'

The scriptwriters listened to Josh and were able to make it more over-the-top. He was really happy with the way things went and says the Josh Groban we see in 'Acafellas' is definitely more forward than the real him.

Powerhouse singer Amber Riley plays Mercedes Jones.

just two years old and her mother was shocked at how quickly she could pick up new songs. Little Amber would simply copy whatever her mother sang. Her mother encouraged her from that day on to keep singing and gave her singing lessons too.

Amber first performed in front of an audience when she was four years old. She can't remember what she sang, but remembers the applause she got and that it was in a park.

A few years later when she was seventeen, Amber decided the time was right for her to get a recording contract. It's really hard to land such a deal because so many people want to be singers and each record label only has space for a few new artists each year. But Amber knew singing was her passion and sent off her application for *American Idol* Season 2 hoping that she would soon follow in the footsteps of Kelly Clarkson, who won Season 1.

American Idol ended up being a big letdown for Amber as she only made it to the producers' round. She didn't even get to perform for Simon Cowell, Paula Abdul or Randy Jackson as the producers' round picks out the singers who are either brilliant or totally rubbish to put forward for the televised audition with the judges. Sadly, Amber didn't make the cut and whoever failed to notice her amazing voice must be kicking themselves now because she would have been a real contender in the live finals.

Amber was devastated to be told that her *American Idol* dreams were over, but insists she learned a lot from the experience and it made her stronger. Years later, when she was auditioning for various other projects, she was able to let negative comments and rejections not hurt her. She just kept on going, knowing that her big break would surely come one day.

When she was at school, Amber wasn't in many of the clubs because she was too busy trying to build a singing career. As she explained to the *Wall Street Journal*: 'I kind of had a life outside of high school. I was singing in background, singing in choir, studio work. There wasn't a Glee club in my school, and if there was I sincerely apologise, I had no idea.'

At the age of sixteen, Amber did a pilot for *St. Sass*, which didn't impress enough people to be made into a series which was another blow for her but she quickly landed a part in a comedy sketch show called *Cedric the Entertainer Presents*. She also managed to build up a successful theatre career before *Glee* came along and turned her life upside down.

Glee is such a unique show that Amber didn't fully understand what it was all about when she attended her first audition. She was actually very fortunate to get the role of Mercedes because she was one of the last people to audition. Amber wrongly thought that Mercedes was a small part and she'd be doing background singing; she didn't realise she'd have to show off her acting and dancing skills in the audition as well. She must have been shocked when she was handed some sides to read. Amber also recognised Ryan Murphy (one of the creators of *Glee*) because he had been one of the writers on *Cedric the Entertainer Presents*.

Amber revealed what happened on the Fox video 'Up Close with Amber Riley': 'When I came into the first audition (Ryan Murphy's) mouth dropped and his eyes were wide open when he found out I could sing because he didn't know I could. He asked me to sing a song from *Dreamgirls* and I was completely mortified and terrified because I had never ever sung that song before, but ended up having a wonderful time.'

Amber's audition was so good that the casting director knew within two lines of 'And I Am Telling You I'm Not Going' that she would be the perfect Mercedes. It was one of the most exciting audition moments he has ever experienced. Wow!

Looking back, Amber is so glad the audition went well and she got the part. She feels that God has truly blessed her and it's all happened so fast: one day she was just plain old Amber Riley and now she's an international megastar with millions of fans. She really is living out her dreams in *Glee*.

Having already been in several plays and theatre productions helped Amber when she started on *Glee* as she was used to a demanding schedule and learning lines in a short period of time. Doing live theatre also builds your stamina. Amber might only be in her early twenties but she has performed in productions of *Into the Woods*, *Alice in Wonderland*, *A Midsummer Night's Dream* and *Mystery on the Docks*. She loved her theatre work, so may go back one day. Lots of successful actors and actresses do plays, TV shows and movies.

Glee fans love Amber because she is always smiling and her bubbly personality shines through during interviews. She would be a great friend to any girl as she has a fantastic sense of humour and loves shopping!

Amber celebrated getting her first *Glee* paycheck by buying three pairs of Louis Vuitton heels. She's a girl who loves shoes so much that she calls them her 'babies' and when she's travelling across America and the world by plane she carries them in her purse – she doesn't want to pack them in her suitcase in case something happens to them. In total, she has over 100 pairs of shoes!

As well as shoe shopping, Amber enjoys buying clothes and accessories with Chris Colfer (Kurt). Like her character Mercedes, she likes to wear nice clothes but she doesn't feel the need to tell everyone how much everything cost and where she got it from. She admires Mercedes' confidence, but doesn't feel that she herself can carry off some of the bold outfits that her character wears in the show.

When she's out shopping she loves visiting Target stores but she has set herself a $100 limit per visit with Chris – he loves Target too. They also like visiting the latest boutiques and stores where they can look at new stuff that they haven't seen before. Amber's current wardrobe is a real mix of designer and bargain fashion items. She likes being fashionable, but believes that being comfortable is also important.

Even celebrities get starstruck at times and Amber is no different. She felt like she was going to pass out on the TV talk show *Good Day LA* when she was asked to sing alongside Motown legend Stevie Wonder. Another celebrity that Amber loves is Queen Latifah but she hasn't yet managed to meet the Grammy Award winning actress, rapper and singer. She recently found out that Queen Latifah's brother is her neighbour so she keeps on checking to see if Queen Latifah is in her hallway. Very funny!

Hopefully Amber will get her wish to meet Queen Latifah soon. It would be really nice if she could make a guest appearance on *Glee* and maybe sing a duet with Amber.

Amber is such a great singer because she is passionate about music. The cast has nicknamed her the 'human iTunes' because she always knows the songs when they get their scripts even if the rest of the crew don't. She readily admits that she prefers classic songs rather than the new ones artists are producing today. The album she likes best is *Continuum* by John Mayer and his song 'Gravity' is her favourite song. It is constantly on her iPod – she listens to it about 20 times a day.

If Amber was in charge of the music for one episode of *Glee* she would pick 'Boom Boom Pow' by the Black Eyed Peas. She loves that song and would relish the opportunity to perform it on *Glee*. Her special guest would be Patti LaBelle because she is one of the *Glee* star's favourite singers of all time. She would also like the opportunity to showcase some songs she has written herself. Amber sure is one talented lady!

Amber and her cast mates love music and singing so much that they sing between takes. They have been given their own little soundproof area to go into, where they can sing their hearts out without disturbing anyone else. Amber is much less passionate about dancing.

Performing the dance routines take after take is really hard-going for Amber and the rest of the *Glee* cast because there are so many musical numbers in each episode. Every member of the cast has to fully commit to keep on going even when they are too tired. If someone starts to struggle, other members of the crew step in and help them. No one wants to let the team down.

Amber admitted to *The TV Chick*: 'Getting used to the dancing every day, that was the greatest challenge. But we got used to it – we have a really great choreographer,

AMBER IS GREAT PALS WITH CASTMATE CHRIS COLFER.

Zach Woodlee and his assistant Brooke Lipton, and they're really wonderful: they're good with us, they make sure that we know what we're doing, they make us look good, they know what looks good on our bodies, so we're confident when we go up and film.'

Amber is living proof that you can be a big girl and still dance. She's an inspiration for other plus-size women and girls as she's made it in Hollywood without having to be a size zero.

In a recent interview, the editor of the 'Young, Fat & Fabulous' blog asked Amber if she had noticed any pressure in Hollywood because of her larger size. She replied: 'I actually noticed it more when I was younger which is why I stopped – it was getting to my self-esteem. But once I learned I am not my dress size and to never let anyone put me in a box, I was more content with being myself and letting the world see my light shine.'

Amber then added her own fashion tip for plus-sized fans: 'I would say make sure that what you wear makes you feel beautiful and comfortable, dress for your shape, and put a little colour in your life – you'd be surprised how much it can brighten up your day!'

In *Glee* Season 2, Amber hopes that fans will get to see what Mercedes' family is like and how it is for her when she gets home from school. She isn't too fussed about Mercedes getting a boyfriend because she thinks there's already enough dating drama in *Glee*.

She has so many happy memories from filming and promoting *Glee* that she can't really pick a favourite, but seeing the first advert for *Glee* on TV was very special for Amber and her family. It was the moment when she realised that she was going to be a TV star.

Spending time with her family has always been important to Amber and her favourite place in the whole world is sitting on the couch in her living room. At Christmas time, she was more interested in catching up with her mother than going to celebrity parties. Amber is definitely no diva!

Artie Abrams (Played By Kevin McHale)

Artie Abrams is a member of New Directions. He is played by the super talented Kevin McHale.

Artie was in a car crash when he was eight years old, which has left him needing to use a wheelchair all the time. He's the Glee club geek and loves playing his guitar when he's not being chased by bullies from the football team.

Artie loves being in New Directions because it gives him a sense of freedom and a way of escaping his personal problems. He likes doing wheelies in his wheelchair and beat boxing. Even though he is paralysed from the waist down, he still likes playing Dance Dance Revolution. Because he can't use his feet, he just uses his hands.

Playing Artie is quite a big challenge for Kevin McHale because he has to keep his legs and feet still at all times. This would be hard for any able-bodied actor, but because Kevin has always been a dancer, it's even tougher – listening to music makes him want to tap his feet.

Artie is a character that has split a lot of people down the middle. Some disabled groups think that it's great that finally a disabled character is allowed to take centre stage and not let his disability rule his life. Others are angry that the part did not go to a disabled actor because they believe the show's bosses might have been

KEVIN McHALE
PLAYS ARTIE ABRAMS.

too concerned that having a disabled actor would slow down production. But this wasn't the case at all: Kevin was cast because of his natural singing and performing abilities. He showed so much potential in his first audition that it would have been foolish of the *Glee* casting team to let him slip through the net just because he didn't have a disability. It would have also been a kind of prejudice.

Auditions

Ryan Murphy was the man in charge of finding the perfect cast for *Glee* and boy, did he do a good job! Others helped, but Ryan was the one who singled out the right people for the roles. Naturally, no one involved with *Glee* wanted the show to be mediocre and so Ryan had to make sure he signed up talented actors and actresses who could sing, act *and* dance. They all had to be naturally gifted in all three. It was no use having a Rachel Berry who could act and sing, but couldn't dance or a Finn Hudson who could act and dance, but couldn't hold a tune. They needed the best – so Ryan went to Broadway.

Glee meant everything to Ryan because he was one of its three creators. He spent three months on Broadway and came back with his stars.

He found his perfect Will Schuester in Matthew Morrison. Matthew had played Link Larkin in *Hairspray* and Lt. Cable in *South Pacific* on Broadway and also starred in several other big plays and movies. He picked two cast members from *Spring Awakening* to be in *Glee*: Lea Michele was the perfect Rachel Berry and Ryan knew Jenna Ushkowitz would be a great Tina Cohen-Chang.

Chris Colfer (Kurt Hummel) had the shortest résumé of all the *Glee* cast members as he had only finished high school himself a year before shooting the pilot. He wasn't a Broadway star, but the casting director was so impressed that he told Ryan about him and a new role was created just for him.

The other actors who were desperate to be in *Glee* were allowed to audition even if they hadn't been on Broadway, but they had to prove they had all three talents that Ryan and the rest of the creators were looking for.

Jayma Mays gave everything she had during her performance of 'Touch-a, Touch-a, Touch Me' from *The Rocky Horror Show* and was delighted when she was told that she would be playing Emma Pillsbury. Kevin McHale had been in a boy band called Not Like Them so he had to show off his acting skills in his audition in order to land the part of Artie Abrams. Cory Monteith's first audition was different because it wasn't in person. Instead he sent a tape showcasing his acting skills while playing drums with plastic tubs and glasses.

It sounds very odd but it made him stand out and he was asked to submit a second tape. This contained his own take on REO Speedwagon's 'Can't Fight This Feeling', which impressed Ryan so much that he had to meet him. A short time after that, Cory got the good news he was waiting for: he was to play *Glee* heartthrob Finn Hudson.

Most probably, the best thing Ryan did was to cast Jane Lynch as Sue Sylvester. The comedian, actress and writer is a legend and her performance in *Glee* is one of the reasons why people fell in love with the series straight away. No one could have played the part any better than Jane.

On the 11 January 2010, *Glee* fans around the world were stunned into silence when it was announced that the producers would be holding open auditions for three new characters. Anyone aged between sixteen and twenty-six could apply for an audition, whether they had been to acting school or not. Age was the only restriction.

Ryan Murphy declared: 'Anybody and everybody now has a chance to be on a show about talented underdogs. We want to be the first interactive musical comedy on television.'

The three new characters for Season 2 were a rival for Rachel, a love interest for Kurt and a 'Male Mercedes'.

Awards

Every actor and actress on the planet dreams of collecting a big award at the Golden Globes and most have to wait many years for the opportunity to be nominated, let alone win. However, less than a year after the pilot aired, *Glee* won a Golden Globe – what an amazing achievement!

Glee won another seven awards and was nominated for a further fourteen only a few episodes into its first season. Who knows how many awards it will win in the next few years when each episode seems to be getting better and better?

Glee's crew, individual actors and the whole ensemble cast have been nominated for various awards proving that the success of *Glee* is a team effort. It's a dream come true as they just made a small show that became an overnight success. Sadly they didn't win individual Golden Globe trophies, but instead have to share the one Golden Globe. Maybe next year they'll win even more. Whatever happens, it looks like *Glee* will be more successful than *Friends*, which took nine years to win its one and only Golden Globe. Despite only winning one Golden Globe, *Friends* has been constantly on our screens even though the last episode aired on 6 May 2004. There is a strong possibility that *Glee* re-runs could be equally popular over the next decade.

LEA MICHELE GIVES HER
SCREEN ACTORS GUILD
AWARD A BIG SMOOCH!

B is for...

'Bad Reputation' – Season 1, Episode 17

The seventeenth episode of *Glee* is called 'Bad Reputation': it premièred in the USA on 4 May 2010 and first hit the UK screens on 10 May 2010.

In this episode, Sue is made a laughing stock when Kurt and his pals decide to post up a YouTube video of her dancing to Olivia Newton-John's 'Physical'. Sue isn't used to having people laugh at her and to get her own back, she gives Principal Figgins a list that ranks members of New Directions on how sexually promiscuous they are. He in turn is horrified by the 'Glist' and tells teacher Will Schuester that he must find out who wrote the list, or he will close down the

OLIVIA NEWTON JOHN GUEST STARRED IN THE EPISODE 'BAD REPUTATION'.

Glee Club and suspend every member. Will informs New Directions of what will happen if the culprit doesn't come forward; he also sets them the week's task – to sing a song with a bad reputation and transform it into something better. He shows them how it's done by singing Vanilla Ice's 'Ice Ice Baby'.

Meanwhile, Sue can't even get herself a drink of coffee without being made to feel like a fool. Her colleagues can't stop laughing at her and she's insulted by new teacher Brenda Castle but after school, she visits her sister and Jean manages to make her smile again when she reminds Sue that when they were children and felt hurt, they would help out at an animal shelter – it made them realise there are always others less fortunate than themselves. This gives Sue the idea of becoming Emma Pillsbury's therapist and when she eventually gets the chance to speak to Emma on her own, she tells her that Will has been unfaithful.

She tells Emma that she bribed Will Schuester's landlord to bug his apartment with baby monitors placed under his sofa and in his bedroom. She makes Emma stand up for herself and confront Will in front of the other members of staff.

Principal Figgins might be shocked that the 'Glist' exists but Tina, Kurt, Mercedes and Artie are equally shocked that they are not even on the list; Brittany also feels down because she didn't make the top three. The five of them decide they need to build up their bad reputations and so they sneak into the school library and burst into an energetic performance of MC Hammer's 'U Can't Touch This'. They think the librarian will hit the roof, but she actually applauds them and asks if they will perform at her church's Sunday service.

Kurt decides that its time he confessed to Sue that he was the one who posted her video on YouTube. But instead of exploding with rage, Sue thanks him because Olivia Newton-John saw the clip, contacted her and asked her to perform in a remake of 'Physical'. Sue delights in telling staff that she is now one of the top 700 recording artists as the new 'Physical' has been released.

Meanwhile, after grovelling to Emma and giving her some flowers, Will spots Quinn looking upset and he guesses that she is the creator of the 'Glist'. After a heart-to-heart in the rehearsal room, she confesses to

MOLLY SHANNON APPEARED AS BRENDA CASTLE, THE ASTRONOMY TEACHER AT WILLIAM MCKINLEY HIGH, FOR THE FIRST TIME IN THE EPISODE 'BAD REPUTATION'.

him. The deadline to discover the creator of the 'glist' has come and Principal Figgins appears. Instead of telling him it was Quinn, Will decides to protect her and says that no one has come forward, but no new lists have been posted and suggests they forget all about it.

Rachel asks Puck if he will help her create a video for 'Run Joey Run'. Later, when she presents the video to the other members of New Directions, it is clear that she has been working on gaining a bad reputation for herself. Instead of just having Puck as her love interest in the video, she has also used Jesse and Finn – and has edited them all together. All three react badly as they are shocked that Rachel has used them in this way. In fact, Jesse breaks up with her and leaves. The episode ends with Rachel singing 'Total Eclipse of the Heart' on her own.

The guest star in this episode was Olivia Newton-

John, who played herself. This is the first time that we get to meet new astronomy teacher Brenda Castle, played by Molly Shannon.

In this episode the cast did covers of five songs. They sang 'Ice Ice Baby' by Vanilla Ice, Bonnie Tyler's 'Total Eclipse of the Heart', MC Hammer's 'U Can't Touch This', 'Run Joey Run' by David Geddes and 'Physical' by Olivia Newton-John.

All five numbers are available for download, while 'Physical' and 'Total Eclipse of the Heart' were included on the album *Glee: The Music, Volume 3: Showstoppers*.

'Ballad' – Season 1, Episode 10

The tenth episode of *Glee* is called 'Ballad'. It premièred in the USA on 18 November 2009 and first hit UK screens on 8 March 2010.

In this particular episode Will gets the Glee club to split into pairs and each pair must pick a ballad to sing to each other. Because Matt isn't at Glee club that day, Rachel is left on her own and so Will has to step in and be her partner. Pretty much straight away, Rachel finds herself attracted to the Glee club director. As they duet on 'Endless Love', Will starts to panic when he sees the look in Rachel's eyes. It makes him think back to the last time a student had a crush on him – poor Suzy Pepper ended up in a medically induced coma after she couldn't cope with Will rejecting her.

GORGEOUS SARAH DREW LOOKS MILES DIFFERENT FROM HER CHARACTER SUZY PEPPER ON *GLEE*.

The pairing of Rachel and Will isn't the only one to cause trouble either. Finn feels really uncomfortable singing to Kurt and so he's relieved when Kurt suggests that he imagines that he's singing to his unborn daughter instead. Later, when he is practising at home, his mum walks in on him singing to the ultrasound video and realises that her son must have got Quinn pregnant.

Will is concerned that Rachel is going to end up like Suzy Pepper and so he takes Emma Pillsbury's advice and decides to sing Rachel a mash-up of 'Don't Stand So Close to Me' by The Police and 'Young Girl' by Gary Puckett and The Union Gap. Rachel doesn't take the hint and instead thinks this proves Will has feelings for her.

When Kurt finds out that Quinn's parents have invited Finn round for dinner he helps his friend pick out a suitable outfit and advises him to sing '(You're) Having My Baby' by Paul Anka and Odia Coates. He knows this will cause trouble, but is convinced he'll be the one that Finn turns to.

Puck isn't happy with the way Quinn is freezing him out and tells his ballad partner Mercedes that he is the real father of the baby. Mercedes angrily tells him to back off and that Quinn has decided that Finn is the daddy.

Later, during the meal at the Fabrays, Finn bursts

into song, as planned. Quinn is horrified and her parents are so furious that they kick her out of their home. They can't believe their daughter is pregnant. With nowhere to go, Quinn moves in with Finn and his mum.

During an encounter with Suzy Pepper in the bathroom Rachel realises that her crush on Will is just foolish and that she really doesn't fancy him at all – she's only doing it to try and prove that she's attractive and worth something. Rachel apologises to Will for the way she has behaved and knows that she will never get a crush on a teacher again.

When Kurt finds out what has happened he feels partly responsible for telling Finn to sing to his unborn daughter. He decides to come clean too and tells Finn that he is in love with him. Oh dear!

Despite all the problems that have arisen during the work in pairs, the episode ends on a positive note with the whole Glee club singing Bill Withers' 'Lean on Me' to show Quinn and Finn that they will support them every step of the way.

> ## SET SECRET
>
> The actors who play Quinn and Finn were not allowed to see the rehearsals of 'Lean on Me' and so actually only viewed it for the first time when it was filmed. The tears we see rolling down their cheeks are real ones, as they experience the performance just as their characters would if it was real life and not a TV show.

The guest stars in this episode were actor and country musician Gregg Henry and *NYPD Blue*'s Charlotte Ross, who play Quinn's parents, and *Everwood* star Sarah Drew, who plays Suzy Pepper.

In this episode, the music sung by the Glee cast includes cover versions of 'Crush' by Jennifer Paige, 'Endless Love' by Diana Ross and Lionel Richie, 'Lean on Me' by Bill Withers, 'I'll Stand By You' by The Pretenders and '(You're) Having My Baby' by Paul Anka and Odia Coates. They also do a mash-up of 'Don't Stand So Close to Me' by The Police and 'Young Girl' by Gary Puckett and The Union Gap.

All the songs from this particular episode of *Glee* were released for download. The mash-up of 'Don't Stand So Close to Me' and 'Young Girl' proved the most popular, charting at number 64 in the USA and number 67 in Canada. The second most popular was 'I'll Stand by

You', which achieved number 73 in the USA charts and number 65 in the Canadian charts.

Brad Falchuk

One of the three guys who created *Glee* is TV writer, director and producer Brad Falchuk. Although Ian Brennan came up with the initial idea and wrote *Glee* as a screenplay, it was when Brad and Ryan Murphy got on board that they realised that it would work better as a TV series.

Brad started his TV career in 2001 when he became a writer for the comic book-based series *Mutant X*. He went on to write for the Canadian science fiction TV series *Earth: Final Conflict* and *Veritas: The Quest*, an Indiana Jones-style TV series, before getting his big break in 2003, when he was asked to work on *Nip/Tuck*.

Brad joined *Nip/Tuck* in the first season, before it had received its Golden Globe and five other awards. The series set in a plastic surgery practice propelled him to the top and allowed him to work with Ryan Murphy, who was the producer. Together, they wrote a pilot for a new TV series called *Pretty/Handsome*, but it was never made into a series.

Both Brad and Ryan loved working on *Nip/Tuck* so much that during the final season of the hit show they decided they needed to have another project to work on

MARK SALLING WITH
BRAD FALCHUK *(RIGHT)*.

together. They wanted to try something new that they hadn't done before and jumped at the chance to work with screenwriter Ian Brennan on a screenplay about high-school choirs. The three men pitched their idea to Fox Broadcasting Company, following which *Glee* was given the thumbs-up.

Brad must have been so proud when the *Glee* pilot premièred and became an instant hit. Almost certainly, he had no idea when he sat down with his friends Ryan and Ian to write the first proper *Glee* script just how popular their series would become or how audiences across the globe would fall in love with their characters and storylines.

A lot of what happens in *Glee* comes from Brad and the other *Glee* creators' own experiences in high school. Brad admitted to Wired.com: 'The point of the show is that every teenager is a geek. Every teenager feels a wanting, a desire for something more, to be heard, to be seen. In reality, I was more of the Finn/Puck type in high school (yes, we did throw a kid in the dumpster a few times) but like those characters I was unsure of myself and my place. I think the show is working for people of all ages, though, because that feeling never really goes away.'

Brad recognises that the success of *Glee* is not solely down to the script but because the actors themselves have made the series such a hit. He especially loves writing for Chris Colfer (Kurt) because he finds him hilarious; also, he can throw anything at him and Chris will do it.

If Brad was going to get up and sing at a karaoke bar he would pick Amber (Mercedes) or Lea (Rachel) to join him because they are such talented artists and he could just blend into the background.

Brittany (Played By Heather Morris)

Brittany is one of the Cheerios cheerleaders and a good friend of Quinn Fabray. She joins the Glee club in episode 2, 'Showmance'.

We will have to wait until Season 2 to learn more about Brittany and her family history as her character hasn't really been developed in Season 1. All we know is that she is Dutch and seems a bit dim.

The first impression we get of Brittany is that she's quite sly and manipulative like Quinn and Santana, but as Season 1 develops we realise she's just misguided and isn't so bad after all.

When Will buys New Directions wigs he needs someone to show Rachel, Chris and the rest of the glee club how hairography works. Brittany is the perfect teacher.

In many ways it's easy to say that Brittany is just a stereotypical dumb blonde, but she's much more than that.

HEATHER MORRIS,
WHO PLAYS BRITTANY.

Chris Colfer

The youngest member of the *Glee* cast is Chris Colfer, who plays the lovable Kurt. Chris might not have had much acting experience before *Glee*, but judging from his acting ability and fan base, he will be in demand for many years to come. He is one of the favourites to be a big movie star in the future alongside Lea Michele, who also shows great potential.

Chris has always loved performing and says he loved performing even when he was in him mum's womb. No other job would satisfy him because acting, singing and dancing is all he's ever wanted to do. He was in lots of plays and musical productions at school

CHRIS COLFER
HAS STOLEN THE
SPOTLIGHT WITH
HIS INCREDIBLE
TURN AS KURT
IN GLEE.

and in his local area. When he was just fourteen years old, he helped direct a show for Valley Children's Hospital. As well as acting and directing, he is a keen writer and was president of his school's writers club before he graduated.

Chris's audition for *Glee* was really nerve-wracking: he explained what happened to the *Los Angeles Times*. After he walked into the audition room, the *Glee* executive producer said: 'Why do I have the feeling you've been Rolf on *The Sound of Music* before?' Chris smiled and replied: 'I know, I have Von Trapp written all over me! I actually was Kurt in *The Sound of Music* a long time ago.'

Poor Chris was feeling so nervous that he dropped his script pages all over the floor and had to pick them up.

He told the paper: 'I was thinking, "I can't do this. I can't sing and dance in front of this man." I idolize him so much. So I immediately peed a little. I'm horrible at auditions anyway. Maybe that's why I never got anything – it's my Achilles' heel.'

When he opened his mouth to sing the song 'Mr. Cellophane' from *Chicago* everyone in the audition room must have known that they had found a star. Chris has the most beautiful voice.

Creator Ryan Murphy knew straight away that Chris was special: 'He's never been formally trained and I just thought he was so talented and gifted and unusual. I've never seen anyone who looks like him or acts like him, or sounds like him. You'd think he'd been at Juilliard for six years, but he hasn't.'

Originally, Chris went up against Kevin McHale for the part of Artie Abrams but he didn't get it. Instead, the creators of the show invented the character of Kurt, which would suit his personality and musical abilities better.

Cory Monteith (who plays Finn) might be seen by many as the biggest heartthrob in *Glee* but Chris has just as many fans. Girls always approach him in the street for autographs and simply to say hello. He explained what it's like to *Entertainment Weekly*: 'I was at Disneyland yesterday – big mistake. I might as well have walked around with a target on my shirt, because those are our fans. I stopped and took pictures, probably 40 times in between rides. This one lady got a picture of me on the Tower of Terror and had me sign it.'

Chris is so famous that he can't leave his own home without fans following him everywhere! The series is now a worldwide hit, so even if he decided to go abroad on holiday, he would probably bump into a *Glee* fan or two.

It's not only fans of the show who love Chris but even the actors and actresses who work alongside him think he's great. Amber Riley (Mercedes in the show) adores

Chris and is his biggest fan. She loves hanging out with him and thinks he's a fantastic entertainer.

If you happen to be a big Chris fan and want to keep up-to-date with his latest news and movements, you need to follow him on Twitter. He has over 90,000 people following him already, proof indeed that he really is a big star now. If you don't live in the USA, you might think that you won't ever get the opportunity to meet him but you never know, there could be an international *Glee* tour one day. Chris would love to get

Chris Colfer and Jenna Ushkowitz grab some lunch.

to know more of his fans and when he was asked by GleeFan.com which country he would most like to visit, he replied: 'How could I only pick one? England, France, and Black Forest Germany. I'd also like to go skiing on the Matterhorn in Switzerland and eat my weight in pasta in Italy. Knowing me, I'd probably sneak over to Austria and find the *Sound of Music* filming locations.'

Filming Season 1 of *Glee* was a great experience for Chris and he has so many good memories to look back on. He will never forget the episode 'Wheels' because it was so tough being in a wheelchair and having to dance too, but enjoyable at the same time. All the New Directions' actors found it hard going, practising in their wheelchairs for 18 hours a day as they went over their musical number again and again. Poor Amber fell out of her chair and Naya Rivera (Santana) cut her thumb.

Chris believes the 'Wheels' episode allowed *Glee* to deal with lots of sensitive issues in a good and positive way. Fans loved it too and appreciate all the hard work the cast must have put in to make sure the musical number looked slick. Chris also loved the 'Wheels' episode because it gave him the opportunity to sing 'Defying Gravity.' He explained to TVGuide.com: 'It is my favorite song of all time and the fact that I got to perform it is a complete dream come true. The fact that I had to sing against Lea was extremely nerve-racking because I don't know if you know this, but she has a good voice. She's kind of a power house.'

If you love Chris, don't be fooled into thinking he's just like Kurt. Like anyone else, he is his own person and has to act his character – he can't just turn up on set and be himself. As he explained to GleeFan.com: 'One of the biggest misconceptions is that I am Kurt. It's hard convincing people I'm not when the role was written for me and the media begins to focus so much on our similarities. But I don't mind it. I wish I was more like him. I'm more of a mix between Rachel and Sue (determined, nerdy, perfectionist, with lots of inappropriate witty remarks that make Amber punch me in the shoulder). I've noticed I've started picking up some of Kurt's traits (crossing the legs when I sit, standing with one hip out). That's what you get when you pretend to be someone else all day!'

Cory Monteith

Canadian Cory Monteith plays the *Glee* heartthrob Finn Hudson. Unlike many of the other actors and actresses in *Glee*, Cory hasn't always been able to be a full-time actor. In between roles, he has had to take on many different jobs to support himself. He has been a people greeter in a supermarket, a school bus driver, changed oil and tyres, drove a taxi and for a while was a roofer doing construction work.

It was during his time as a taxi driver and roofer that someone suggested that he should become an actor. Cory told E! News: 'I was at a loose end and somebody said, "You should be an actor!" I was like, "Sure! I need to pay my rent."'

Glee fans owe the person who suggested that Cory's career should change so much. If they hadn't said something, then he would probably still be scraping a living in a small town in Canada instead of living a life people only dream about in Los Angeles.

Cory's first acting job was back in 1994 on the sci-fi TV series, *Stargate: Atlantis*. He was twenty-one years old. Since then he has had small parts in *Smallville* and *Supernatural*, plus several other TV shows, generally appearing in just one episode for each show. His first movie role was when he played Kahill in *Final Destination 3*. It wasn't one of the main parts, so Cory wasn't able to show off his acting ability. *Glee* really was the big turning point for him because for once he was in the foreground as one of the main characters instead of being stuck at the back with only a handful of lines.

Cory is a real inspiration to actors who are struggling with bit parts because it would have been so easy for him to give up acting and try and do something else instead.

THE GORGEOUS CANADIAN ACTOR CORY MONTEITH HAS HIT THE BIG TIME WITH *GLEE*.

If he hadn't persisted with it, he would have missed out on the opportunity of a lifetime.

He revealed to journalist Sarah Kuhn how he got the part of Finn: 'I sent an audition tape from Canada. That was the first time I'd ever auditioned and sung; I'd never done anything like that before. I'd never sent a tape of myself singing; I'd never sung for anybody. My agent hooked me up with [*Glee* musical director] Brad Ellis, 'cause he was the guy who was going to be the piano accompaniment for the auditions. So I spent a couple hours with him on the weekend before the test, and I said, "This is the song I want to sing. Can you teach me how to sing it?" I had no idea what I was doing. I thought they wanted musical theater, so I was going to sing a song from *Rent*. We chose different songs after working together; it ended up being Billy Joel.'

All Cory's hard work paid off and he got the part!

Cory is a big Twitter fan and likes to interact with his fans in this way. His Twitter profile reads: 'tall, awkward, canadian, actor, person'. Sometimes he makes mistakes when he tweets, as Chris Colfer explained to one journalist. He said that Cory once revealed which restaurant they were eating at and 40 fans turned up. Now Cory is much more wary and still posts private things, but doesn't reveal his exact location so he can go about his everyday life without being bombarded by fans wanting autographs and photos 24/7.

As well as keeping *Glee* fans up-to-date with his personal news, Cory also tries to help people out, too. A singer from San Francisco called Manny Garcia did a really great mash-up of two *Glee* tracks and Cory was so impressed that he tweeted about it and gave his fans a link to the video on YouTube. Within a few hours the video had been viewed over 25,000 times and Cory's fans were retweeting the link too. Manny instantly got the exposure that every artist desires, thanks to Cory and his Twitter account.

Working on *Glee* has been an awesome experience for Cory, and much more enjoyable than he probably expected when he first got the part of Finn. First time around, he was never a fan of high school and dropped out in ninth grade. It seems unlikely that he will ever continue his studies and graduate now that he is a big star.

Being in *Glee* made Cory realise how much fun it can be at high school – something he never experienced when he was younger. He explained to E! News: 'It wasn't for me. I can remember ever since about the sixth or seventh grade, I just didn't understand why I had to learn what I was learning. For some reason, there was a spirit of rebellion in me.'

In the future, Cory would like to be a movie star and maybe take on roles of darker characters older than

CORY LOVES TO INTERACT WITH HIS FANS.

he is. Cory is a lot older in real life than the character he plays in *Glee*. He was twenty-six when he started filming *Glee* – and is only four years younger than Matthew Morrison, who plays Will Schuester, his teacher.

If Cory had to pick one actor whose footsteps he would like to follow in, then it would be Alec Baldwin. He admires the career choices his fellow actor has made, but also likes the fact that Alec is a keen activist in real life when he's not filming movies.

CORY MIGHT NOT DRINK ALCOHOL BUT HE LOVES HIS STARBUCKS!

DID YOU KNOW...?

Cory is teetotal: he thinks not drinking alcohol allows him to focus on his acting career and what he is doing. He believes that if he drank then the shift of focus could be damaging and he really doesn't want to become one of those celebrities who have to be carried out of clubs when they have had too much. It sounds unlikely that he will ever have to book himself into rehab unlike so many other young stars who develop addictions to drink and drugs.

Now that Cory is famous, many companies try and give him stuff for free but he doesn't always want or need what they offer him. Unlike other celebrities who take whatever they can get, he isn't afraid to say no. He loves wearing flip-flops with shorts, but he only took a single pair when offered 27 pairs by one company.

Cory had to leave his family and friends behind in Canada when he made the move to Los Angeles to advance his acting career. He confided in a journalist from E! News: 'People are really happy that it worked out. Things went very, very badly in my life for a long time and now they are going very well. I don't forget where I come from.'

He is definitely right – in fact, right now things couldn't be going any better for the real-life Finn Hudson. His looks have landed him a deal with Five Four Clothing, who are using him to promote their brand in its winter advertising campaign. Cory looks so sexy as he poses for the camera in various different outfits. As his fan base grows, he will no doubt be asked to appear in adverts for big designer brands, just as David Beckham and Matthew McConaughey do for Armani and Dolce & Gabbana.

The fact that he was famous hit Cory all of a sudden when the first *Glee* soundtrack was released, back in November 2009. He told The TV Addict: 'We were at

Columbus Circle just up the street from here and we came down an escalator, and how loud people were screaming to see the cast of *Glee* was remarkable. And we were all like – I remember looking at Lea Michele and we looked at each other and we were like... Things have changed a lot in the last little while.'

Working on such a top show has allowed Cory and the rest of the cast to rub shoulders with a lot of famous faces that have guest-starred on *Glee*. One interviewer asked Cory who had been his favourite. He replied: 'Oh, it's hard to pick favourites! I don't know – Victor Garber is incredibly talented and [great] to work with. Kristin Chenoweth is such a pro. Everybody's been great, we have not had a bad experience.'

It is clear in every interview Cory gives that he is passionate about *Glee* and its musical numbers. He really loves singing so those scenes are his favourites: he thinks the songs are always spot-on, but he would like to sing something by REO Speedwagon or Journey if he could, because he thinks they would suit Finn down to the ground. Some members of the cast weren't looking forward to filming the episode with all the Madonna tracks because they didn't really know that many of her songs, but Cory was keen. He thought singing Madonna songs would be a 'really great experience'.

Virtually every female who is a fan of *Glee* would love to be Cory's girlfriend. They can't believe that he is

CORY IS ALWAYS THE SUBJECT OF RELATIONSHIP GOSSIP, INCLUDING THE RUMOUR OF HIM DATING COUNTRY MUSIC SENSATION TAYLOR SWIFT.

still single. Women must be throwing themselves at him all the time, but he isn't dating. If you think you could be his perfect woman then you might like to know what he looks for in a partner. He revealed to The TV Addict: 'I think intelligence is a wonderful quality. I think passion. I think people who are interested in what they are doing, and passionate about what they are doing is very attractive.'

If that sounds like you, why not send him a message on Twitter?

D is for...

Dianna Agron

Glee's head cheerleader Quinn Fabray is played by Dianna Agron: as soon as she read the pilot script, she knew that she had to play Quinn and so she sent the casting director an amazing video. In it she sang the Frank Sinatra classic 'Fly Me to the Moon' – an unusual choice considering it is generally regarded as a man's song, and came out in 1964. Other girls might have picked a Pink or Britney number, but not Dianna. She chose a song that would showcase her talent and make her stand out from the crowd.

In the second part of her video audition she displayed her acting skills by pretending that the

BEAUTIFUL
DIANNA AGRON
ALWAYS LOOKS
PERFECT ON THE
RED CARPET.

camera was Finn and read some of Quinn's lines from the pilot. The video audition was such a big success that it resulted in her getting a face-to-face audition soon afterwards.

Glee wasn't the first television series where Dianna appeared as a cheerleader. She played mean cheerleader Debbie Marshall in *Heroes* alongside Hayden Panettiere and Milo Ventimiglia. In fact, Dianna has worked with Milo (who plays Peter Petrelli) in a TV mini-series called *It's a Mall World* in 2007, too. She has also been in the TV shows *Veronica Mars*, *Numb3rs*, *Close to Home*, *Shark* and *CSI: NY*.

Because Dianna naturally looks like a cheerleader, people often wrongly presume she was one when she was in high school and that she was Little Miss Popular too, but that wasn't the case.

She told Hitfix: 'I definitely wasn't cool in high school, I really wasn't. I did belong to many of the clubs and was in leadership on yearbook and did the musical theater route, so I had friends in all areas, but I certainly did not know what to wear, did not know how to do my hair, all those things.

'I've been dancing since I was three – ballet and jazz and hip-hop eventually – but I didn't have time [to be a cheerleader]. It wasn't even something that I had time to think about wanting to do.'

Working on *Glee* has given Dianna an insight into

how hard cheerleaders have to work. She thinks they do a great job and has a lot of respect for them. While filming the *Glee* pilot, she hurt her knee coming down from one of the lifts but thankfully it was only a strain and she didn't do herself any lasting injury.

Dianna is a big supporter of PETA (People for the Ethical Treatment of Animals) and doesn't eat meat. She is not just a pretty face and really wants to make a difference in the world: she filmed a YouTube video for cancer charity 'Love Cures Cancer.com' asking people to donate. Dianna is also a good role model for young girls because she doesn't feel the need to go on sun beds or cover herself in fake tan; she doesn't attempt to hide her pale skin at premières or on nights out.

Not many people know this but Dianna is a big fan of cemeteries. Other girls might like going on shopping sprees when they have free time, but Dianna likes to wander round graveyards. She confessed to talk show host George Lopez: 'I find beauty in many things, but particularly, I really love cemeteries, and I was just in Europe and there's some very, very old cemeteries there so there's one in particular where all the graves are from the 1800s, all the graves are sinking into the ground, falling apart. It was gorgeous.'

Asked how she became so fascinated with cemeteries, she replied: 'I find such peace in them, and

DIANNA AND LEA MICHELE LIVE TOGETHER.

there's not usually other people around and it's very tranquil and I take my iPod and I just kind of walk around them.'

Dianna also likes *The Nightmare Before Christmas* director Tim Burton, skeleton drawings, bats and pirates. She currently lives with Lea Michele, who plays her onscreen enemy, Rachel Berry. The girls are great friends and like to throw parties. The whole *Glee* cast live close together so they don't have to travel far to hang out.

Dijon Talton

Football player Matt Rutherford in *Glee* is played by Dijon Talton: he had only been in one film before being cast in the series and that was way back in 1998 when he was just nine years old. The film was called *L.A Without a Map*. Dijon is a very strong singer and dancer, who has appeared in two McDonalds' adverts in the past.

Since filming his first few episodes of *Glee*, Dijon has filmed a movie called *I Will Follow* – he was really excited to be cast and looks forward to the release. He told *Starry Constellation* magazine: 'It's an incredible, incredible story with a great cast and it was an amazing experience. It's about a normal day in a woman's life, not anything spectacular like a wedding day or graduation. It's a simple day when you're

DIJON TALTON
DOESN'T GET AS
MUCH SCREEN TIME
AS HE DESERVES!

packing up some of the pathways home and how that affects the rest of your life, like the interactions she has with her family and friends and people who help her change her course of life forever. It's just a beautiful story about how a simple day can impact you in ways you never thought.

'It's this really cool art-house theater type of film and it has Salli Richardson-Whitfield in it from the show *Eureka*, Blair Underwood, Omari Hardwick, Tracie Thoms from *Cold Case*, and myself. It's a really great cast and a really good director, and the story needs to be told – it's something different, not so cliché.'

Dijon has a special bond with Harry Shum Jr., who plays Mike Chang and Heather Morris (Brittany) because their characters first appeared within an episode or two of each other. He also gets on with the main *Glee* actors too.

He explained: 'We all kind of hung out all of the time because we were always together rehearsing or shooting, or going to eat during lunch hour or going to have a birthday party for someone after work. From day one when we got there it was like open arms, even with Matthew Morrison who plays Mr. Schuester, it was just open arms and just such a great vibe and such a great energy, and it felt like a family atmosphere.'

Dijon liked the fact that the actors who had been on

Glee from the beginning still wanted to get to know and socialise with the newbies even though they were a few episodes in. He stated to one journalist: 'They were excited about what we were going to bring to the show and different opportunities and storylines, and things that could possibly come from these characters joining the Glee club and the show. I do have a strong relationship with Harry and with Heather, but I have a good relationship with pretty much everyone. I love and miss them all, and I look forward to working with them. Dianna is the biggest sweetheart that you'll ever meet and every time you see her, everyday, even though you just saw her ten hours ago, she makes you feel like you haven't seen her in a year. She's so genuine and so real. I look forward to each relationship differently because each brings something different.'

It doesn't sound as if there's a single member of the *Glee* cast who Dijon dislikes. They all seem to be nice, genuine people and no one appears to have a big ego – it must be a lovely set to work on.

Dorothy of Oz

Two members of the *Glee* cast will be lending their voices to a new animated movie due to hit cinemas in 2011. *Dorothy of Oz* follows the story of Dorothy as she returns home to Kansas from Oz and finds that the tornado has wrecked her home and everyone is leaving

KRISTIN CHENOWETH, WHO PLAYED THE CHARACTER OF APRIL IN *GLEE*, WILL STAR WITH LEA MICHELE IN *DOROTHY OF OZ*.

town. She then gets transported back to Oz and sees that it has been completely ruined too and her friends are missing: she must go on a journey to find the Scarecrow, Tin Man and Cowardly Lion. The movie is based on the book, *The Wonderful Wizard of Oz* by L. Frank Baum.

Lea Michele's voice is being used for Dorothy and Kristin Chenoweth will play Dorothy's new friend, the China Doll Princess. Of course, they are very different roles to Rachel Berry and April Rhodes. *Glee* fans are excited for both actresses, but particularly Lea, as they look forward to hearing her perform some amazing new songs. It's just a shame that only her voice is being used because she would make a fantastic real-life Dorothy, too.

'Dream On' – Season 1, Episode 19

The nineteenth episode of *Glee* is called 'Dream On': it premièred in the USA on 18 May 2010 and first hit the UK screens on 24 May 2010.

In this episode, an auditor from the school board arrives to try and decide which club must be cut to save money. Bryan Ryan actually attended William McKinley High and was a member of the Glee Club, but he isn't the biggest fan of New Directions and thinks the Glee Club should fold. He's angry because he himself harboured dreams of becoming a star,

IDINA MENZEL
PLAYS RACHEL'S
MOTHER, SHELBY.
THE RESEMBLANCE
BETWEEN THE TWO
ACTRESSES IS
UNCANNY!

but he never made the big time on graduation. Bryan gets all the members of New Directions to write down their biggest dream, but then takes Artie's piece of paper and throws it in the bin. He tells them that their dreams will never come true and poor Rachel looks like her world has just ended. In response, Will defends his students and tries to make them feel happy again.

Will later gets Bryan on his own and attempts to convince him he could still make it. Together, they sing 'Piano Man' and both audition for the part of Jean Valjean in a local production of *Les Misérables*. Bryan's audition goes so well that he thinks he must have landed the part and he's so excited that he presents the Glee Club with new costumes, only to take them back seconds later when Sue barges in and announces that Will has secured the lead and that Bryan only has one line. Gutted, Bryan announces that he's cutting the club.

Will realises there's only one thing that will save the Glee Club and so he gives up his role to Bryan. Meanwhile, Rachel admits to Jesse that she has always wanted to find out the identity of her mother – her fathers don't talk about her at all and although she doesn't want to upset them, she feels she has to know who her mother is. Jesse suggests they go through the boxes of records that she has in her basement to see if they hold the truth. While Rachel has her back turned, Jesse sneaks a tape into the box and then claims to have found a tape from her mother. (Jesse was actually given the tape by Shelby, the coach of Vocal Adrenaline, who had asked him to get close to Rachel in the first place.) Jesse is surprised when Rachel says she's not ready to listen to the tape and later, when he goes to meet Shelby, he has to break the news to her. In fact, Shelby is Rachel's long-lost mother! She asks Jesse to do what he can to make Rachel listen. Rachel enters the room to hear a beautiful version of 'I Dreamed a Dream' sung by Shelby.

Also in this episode Tina realises that Artie's greatest dream is to be able to dance. She really wants to encourage him and after helping him stand, she thinks they can dance together, only for Artie to fall on the floor and ask her to leave. By way of apology and to show him that she really cares, Tina prints off lots of information about spinal cord injury treatments. This information makes him dream of a day when he will be able to dance and he visits school guidance counsellor Emma for advice. She tries to make him realise that a breakthrough is still years away and so he won't be able to dance in a few weeks or even months. Artie is really upset and tells Tina that she needs to find another dancer to be her partner, but he will sing while they dance.

In this episode, the cast cover seven songs: 'The Safety Dance' by Men Without Hats, Aerosmith's 'Dream On', 'Big Spender' from the musical *Sweet Charity*, 'Piano Man' by Billy Joel, The Monkees' 'Daydream Believer', 'Dream a Little Dream of Me' by The Mamas and the Papas and 'I Dreamed a Dream' from *Les Misérables*.

'The Safety Dance,' 'Dream On', 'Dream a Little Dream of Me' and 'I Dreamed a Dream' were released for download, while 'Dream On', 'The Safety Dance' and 'I Dreamed a Dream' were included on *Glee: The Music, Volume 3: Showstoppers*.

SET SECRETS

Artie's dream sequence was set in a real mall, which meant that the shoppers filmed were just people going about their usual business. Kevin felt under pressure to make sure he mastered the moves but he needn't have worried – he did a great job.

E is for...

Emma Pillsbury (Played By Jayma Mays)

At the high school in *Glee*, Emma Pillsbury is the guidance counsellor and she is played by Jayma Mays.

Emma has a huge crush on Will Schuester, the director of the Glee club, and she'll do anything to help him. Mysophobic, she has been petrified of germs ever since her brother pushed her into a run-off creek filled with faeces and blood when she was young. Because of this bad experience, she constantly washes her hands and is a member of the Western Ohio Disinfectant Society.

Emma is a person who always has a smile on her face and she is very excitable. She likes things to be in their proper place and always makes sure her clothes are

EMMA PILLSBURY IS PLAYED
BY THE LOVELY JAYMA
Mays.

colour-coordinated. Naturally, she realises that she must try to get over Will because he is married and so she starts to date Ken Tanaka, who is the school's football coach. They later get engaged.

Ken is the complete opposite of Will. He tells Emma that, although he's not very experienced with relationships, he is nevertheless a good man who will treat her honourably.

When Emma postpones her wedding so that she can take the Glee club to Sectionals because Will is banned, Ken realises he will never be the one for her and so they split. She realises that she can't work at the school any more so she hands in her resignation but before she can leave, Will catches up with her and they share a kiss.

F is for...

Fans

Ask any member of the *Glee* cast why the show is such a big hit and they will say, 'Because of the fans.' From the pilot episode, it is the fans who have got behind *Glee* and encouraged the actors to want to make each episode as great as they possibly can.

Glee might have not been running on our screens for all that long, but fans already have a nickname – Gleeks. There are dozens of fan sites set up to document each interview a cast member does, summarise each individual episode and allow fans to discuss *everything* *Glee*-related. Social networking sites have played a big part in the mobilisation of *Glee* fans too. As soon as a

FANS TURNED OUT IN DROVES TO CATCH A GLIMPSE OF THE *GLEE* CAST!

fan spots one of the actors in a restaurant or a shopping centre, they tweet about it so others can share their experience and head on down to see their favourite stars. Members of Facebook *Glee* groups continuously swap gossip and photos – indeed, there never seems to be a dull moment for a Gleek.

Glee fans are so passionate that they spend hours perfecting videos based on the musical numbers featured in the series. They post them on YouTube for everyone to view, so they are well worth checking out when you have some spare time. The *Glee* producers know that the fans do this and so they include instrumental versions of the main songs on the *Glee* soundtracks.

Some fans make some really wacky videos that require lots of skill and planning. Superfan Joe Petrowski made 50,000 Christmas lights dance to the tune of *Glee*'s 'Last Christmas' and posted it on YouTube. How cool is that? It must have taken him ages.

The *Glee* actors themselves are amazed at how talented the *Glee* fan base is. Harry Shum Jr. told ClevverTV: 'They are some of the coolest fans coz they enjoy the music and they like everything about it, so it's cool.'

The cast has previously said that they think the Australian *Glee* fans are more enthusiastic and polite than the ones in the USA. In one interview, they joked that Australian fans have better hygiene and buy better presents. USA fans should take what they said with a pinch of salt, though – they were in Australia at the time.

Finn Hudson (Played By Cory Monteith)

Captain of the football team, Finn Hudson is Mr Popular at William McKinley High School. He is dating the head cheerleader and he can dance and sing, too. When he first joins the Glee club, his teammates can't believe it but they soon accept that he likes singing *and* football.

Finn is played by Cory Monteith who is 11 years older in real life than the character he plays: yikes!

Finn's dad was killed during Operation Desert Storm and so he lives with his mum Carole. When his girlfriend Quinn tells him that she is pregnant with his child, Finn doesn't know what to do but he is determined to support her in whatever way he can. But it turns out that Finn isn't the daddy and his best friend Puck has gone behind his back with Quinn.

When Rachel tells Finn the truth he is devastated. He is so angry that Puck has betrayed him that he beats him up during rehearsals. Quinn gets upset and tells Finn that she's sorry, but Puck is the daddy. Finn can't handle this and says he's had it with everyone. He storms out.

The rest of the Glee club go to Sectionals without him, but just when it looks as if they will lose, he turns up to

CORY MONTEITH PLAYS
FINN HUDSON.

save the day. Afterwards, they start dating only to split up. At Regionals, they hook up again. Will it last? Only time will tell.

Friends

The whole *Glee* cast are really good friends and enjoy hanging out. In breaks between scenes, they like to play games together. One of the games they play is called Mafia, in which they have to sit in a circle and try and find out who the killer is. In the UK, this game is often called Wink Murder. They spend a lot of hours playing this game while the crew set up for the next scene. According to the other cast members, Kevin is the champion of Mafia.

Amber Riley told The TV Chick about the cast's close chemistry: 'I think when we first started, we figured out what the workload was going to be like, and how much we were going to be around each other, so we kind of made up in our minds, okay we're going to work at it. Like with any relationship – a working relationship, a friendship – you have to work at that relationship, and we really did. We made it a point to get to know one another, to know how to work, how everyone's work ethic is, and to be sensible to one another.'

Kevin McHale who plays Artie Abrams agrees. He revealed to journalist Jamie Steinberg: 'I don't know if it's normal for casts, but we clicked instantly. We had about three weeks of rehearsal before shooting the pilot and got along like we'd known each other for years. Even when we were done shooting the pilot and we all split up for a while before we found out the show got picked up, we still talked every single day. We're all each other's best friends.'

'Funk' – Season 1, Episode 21

The twenty-first episode of *Glee* is called 'Funk': it premièred in the USA on 1 June 2010 and first hit the UK screens on 7 June 2010.

In this episode, New Directions start to feel the pressure when they see Vocal Adrenaline perform. Jesse has returned to his former club and, after Sue gives them keys, they perform in the auditorium and cover the practice room with toilet paper. Rachel is heartbroken: they are trying to intimidate New Directions and it's working.

Will hates to see his students looking so depressed and so he comes up with the idea of getting them to perform a funk piece. He tells them that Vocal Adrenaline would never be able to perform funk. Mercedes gets excited at the idea, but Quinn feels she deserves a go at performing a funk piece because she is angry and has passion inside her. The next day, she performs 'It's a Man's Man's Man's World' to show

KEVIN MCHALE
LOVES THE REST OF
THE CAST!

everyone how frustrated she feels at being an unmarried teenage mother. As soon as she finishes singing, everyone crowds round her and gives her a hug. Later Mercedes finds her and tells her that she's welcome to leave Puck's house and move in with herself and her mum. Quinn is thrilled.

Also in this episode Will and Terri finalise their divorce and Will tries to seduce Sue: getting Sue to fall for him might be the only way to give her a taste of her own medicine. He compliments her, performs a sexy version of 'Tell Me Something Good' and asks her out on a date. In turn, Sue finds herself strangely attracted to him and is devastated when she is stood up. She rushes off to Will's apartment to find out what happened, but he rejects her and reveals that he's been trying to hurt her all along.

At school, Kurt explains to Will that Sue has cancelled all the Cheerios practices, has withdrawn them from Nationals and hasn't been in school for days. He tells him how damaging it will be for some of the Cheerios – their whole futures depend on them winning Nationals. Will realises that he's the one to blame and so he calls on a bed-ridden Sue at home. He tells her that her Cheerios love and respect her; he also apologises for his behaviour.

Sue returns to her former self and re-enters the Cheerios for the Nationals competition. Will is delighted when he sees them crowned champions on TV, but is less pleased when Sue barges into his apartment with the large trophy and gives Will two options: he can either display the new trophy in the choir room – or kiss her with tongues! Will picks the kiss, but Sue backs out at the last minute and so the trophy is given its own special display cabinet in the choir room instead.

Will thinks that it's wrong that Vocal Adrenaline got away with vandalising the choir room and tries to get New Directions to come up with a revenge plan. It's left up to Puck and Finn to do the dirty work and they slash the tyres of Vocal Adrenaline's Range Rovers. Shelby visits Principal Figgins to demand that he punishes his pupils and he therefore decides to expel them only for Shelby to insist she doesn't want to press charges – she just wants the culprits to pay for the damages. Finn says he and Puck will get a job so that they can pay her back and Principal Figgins decides to let them stay at the school after all.

Finn and Puck start work alongside Terri and Howard at home goods store Sheets-N-Things, but they don't enjoy it. They are instructed to help their former teacher Sandy Ryerson, but when Finn tells him that the product he wants doesn't come in the colour he prefers, he gets annoyed. Later, Terri asks Finn how old he is and she is delighted when he says sixteen. He reminds her a lot of

Will and after promoting him, she tells him that she will help him prepare his funk number.

Rachel was gutted when she saw Jesse perform with Vocal Adrenaline, but she's delighted when he calls to ask her to meet him in the parking lot. As she runs towards him, she fails to notice the other members of Vocal Adrenaline and does well not to burst into tears as they throw eggs at her. Even Jesse cracks an egg on her head before they leave. New Directions can't believe what's happened to Rachel and the way Vocal Adrenaline are trying to bully them. Will calls Jesse and tells him to meet them in the auditorium with the rest of Vocal Adrenaline. New Directions perform an version of 'Give Up the Funk' to a stunned Vocal Adrenaline, who start to feel intimidated as they themselves can't do funk.

This episode features covers of six songs: 'It's a Man's Man's Man's World' by James Brown, Queen's 'Another One Bites the Dust', 'Give Up the Funk (Tear the Roof off the Sucker)' by Parliament, Rufus's 'Tell Me Something Good', 'Loser' by Beck and 'Good Vibrations' by Marky Mark and the Funky Bunch featuring Loleatta Holloway. 'Give Up the Funk' was included on *Glee: The Music, Volume 3: Showstoppers*, while 'Loser' was included on the deluxe edition.

G is for...

Glee

If you didn't already love *Glee* then you wouldn't be reading this book but sometimes it's nice to find out why the actors who star in the show love it so much.

Matthew Morrison (Will) told TVGuide.com: 'It's such an original show. Every now and then, I think there's a show that's just so fresh and you can't compare it to anything like a cop show or a lawyer show. It's its own thing, and that's what makes the show so appealing. And there's so much optimism at a time we need it. It's a true underdog story and we've all been the underdog at some point in our lives.

'There's a certain amount of camp involved in the

show. The reason we get away with so much stuff is because we don't take ourselves too seriously, and that's going to keep going. *Glee* rides a great line where there's this amazing energy but (it) also has these deep emotional moments as well.'

Guest Stars

Glee wouldn't be *Glee* without a great mix of guest stars in recurring or small roles. There have been several Broadway actors and actresses in the hit show. *Jersey Boys'* star John Lloyd Young played a retired wood shop teacher, *Titanic* actor Victor Garber was Will's dad and *Grey's Anatomy's* Debra Monk played his mum.

Other famous faces who have guest-starred in episodes of *Glee* include *Yes, Dear's* Mike O'Malley as Kurt's dad, *Everwood* actress Sarah Drew (Suzy Pepper) and pop star Eve played a rival Glee club coach in two episodes.

If the cast could pick anyone to guest star on the show, Lea Michele would choose Justin Timberlake, Jenna Ushkowitz plumps for comedienne Kristen Wiig and Mark Salling would go for the Jonas Brothers.

Everyone knows that Amber Riley is the biggest prankster on set and when a certain male guest star was appearing she left a love note in his trailer, pretending that Lea had written it. In it, she said that she couldn't wait to film their scene and ended with a big lipstick

MIKE O'MALLEY GUEST
STARS AS KURT'S DAD.

kiss. Lea only found out when the guest star went up to her and told her that they'd got her note. At first she didn't know who had stitched her up, but once she saw the note and the lipstick kiss, she just knew it had to be Amber as she has the biggest lips!

H is for...

'Hairography' – Season 1, Episode 11

The eleventh episode of *Glee* was called 'Hairography'. It premièred in the USA on 25 November 2009 and first hit UK screens on 15 March 2010.

In this episode Will decides to pay a visit to the Jane Addams Academy for girls recently released from juvenile detention because he thinks that Sue Sylvester has stabbed New Directions in the back by passing on information about their musical numbers to their rivals. She had demanded to see his set lists and Will caught Brittany filming one of their practices.

Will is shocked by all the different security checks he has to go through to meet his rival club director Grace

Eve GUEST-STARRED AS THE RIVAL GLEE CLUB COACH FOR JANE ADDAMS ACADEMY, GRACE HITCHENS.

Hitchens. She is really offended that Will could think that she would cheat just so her girls might win. Will feels guilty when she tells him that they have insufficient funds and nowhere to practice. He says that they can practice in the McKinley High music room but once he sees them perform, he thinks New Directions will struggle to beat them. Ever the optimist, Rachel Berry disagrees and tells him that the other Glee club are using 'hairography' to hide the fact that they aren't the best singers and dancers in the world.

Will has an idea and buys New Directions some wigs so they can practise 'hairography' for themselves. Rachel isn't happy about this because she thinks they don't need wigs to be good.

Aside from the Glee club, Quinn is wondering whether giving her daughter to Will's wife would be a good idea after all. She thinks about what it might be

Lea Michele looks radiant at the première of *Glee* after the mid-season hiatus.

Cory Monteith has become an international heartthrob after playing Finn Hudson.

Above: Cory is interviewed for E! along with Dianna Agron.

Right: Cory loves his mini video camera and often posts videos on his Twitter feed.

Above: Lea and Dianna share a fit of giggles.

Below left: Dianna gets glammed up for the Golden Globe Awards.

Below right: Shooting an advertisement for the Op 'Rock Your Shine' campaign. Dianna featured along with Cory Monteith.

Above left: Amber Riley belts out a tune.

Above right: Kevin McHale surrounded by *Glee* cheerios all sporting the classic 'L for loser' sign.

Below: Amber, Chris and Jenna pose together on the red carpet.

Cory and Mark both got in the festive spirit for TJ Maxx's 'Carol-oke' contest in December 2009.

Above: Dianna, Chris and Mark sure do clean up well!

Below: Heather Morris, Dijon Talton and Naya Rivera get gleeky at the première.

Their characters might not get on too well, but Jayma Mays and Jessalyn Gilsig are great friends off screen.

like to raise a child with Puck rather than Finn. After much thought, she tells Terri that she's keeping the baby.

Terri, of course, isn't at all happy – she needs a baby to keep Will. Her sister Kendra comes up with a plan to make Quinn realise that she isn't cut out to be a mother and arranges for her to baby-sit her three sons. Quinn decides to ask Puck to help her babysit so that she can have some one-on-one time with him. She convinces Kurt that he needs to give Rachel a make-over because she knows this will distract Finn.

Quinn feels close to Puck as they babysit the three boys, but her bubble is burst the next day when Santana approaches and tells her that Puck was sending her sexy texts all night. Following this, Quinn decides that her baby deserves a better dad and so adoption might be the best thing for her baby, after all.

When Dalton Rumba, the Glee club director at Haverbrook School for the Deaf finds out that Will has invited Grace's club to practise at McKinley High, he considers his own club to have been snubbed. He quickly arranges for them to perform at McKinley so his kids won't miss out. New Directions perform a hilarious mash-up of 'Hair' and Beyoncé's 'Crazy In Love', with lots of hair-flipping, which leaves those watching thinking they are a little crazy. The Haverbrook Glee club and New Directions then perform a moving version of John Lennon's 'Imagine' together.

Will finally realises that the mash-up of 'Hair' and 'Crazy In Love' with the wigs just won't cut it and decides they don't need to use hairography to beat the Jane Addams Academy and the Haverbrook School for the Deaf Glee clubs. His Glee club students are such talented singers and dancers that they don't need gimmicks. He decides to drop the mash-up in favour of Cyndi Lauper's 'True Colors'.

A spiteful Sue will do anything to make sure that New Directions lose at Sectionals, so she tells the other Glee club directions the names of the two songs they will be singing and encourages them to have their own Glee clubs perform the same numbers.

When Finn shows Rachel that he isn't a fan of her new look she is upset and realises that Kurt did it intentionally. Kurt and Rachel both come to the realisation that the person Finn wants to be with is Quinn and not either one of them.

The guest stars in this episode were rapper Eve as Grace Hitchens and several contestants from the dance competition show, *So You Think You Can Dance*. *Best in Show* actor Michael Hitchcock plays the Haverbrook School for the Deaf Glee club director Dalton Rumba, too.

Altogether, there were eight covers of songs in this episode: 'Bootylicious' by Destiny's Child, 'Imagine' by John Lennon, Dionne Warwick's 'Don't Make Me

Over', 'Papa Don't Preach' by Madonna, 'You're the One That I Want' from Grease, 'True Colors' by Cyndi Lauper and a mash-up of 'Hair' by the cast of *Hair the Musical* and 'Crazy in Love' by Beyoncé Knowles.

All the songs apart from 'You're the One That I Want' were released for download. Three of the hits from the show ('Don't Make Me Over,' 'True Colors' and 'Imagine') made it onto the second *Glee* album, *Glee: The Music, Volume 2.*

INSIDER GOSSIP

Chris and Cory were so glad that it was the Jane Addams Academy girls that had to do the 'Bootylicious' routine and not New Directions. They thought the jump into the splits might ruin their chances of having kids in the future!

Eve told Fox: 'The one thing I do want to learn from that number is the handstand and the booty shake. I'm gonna figure that out. I'm gonna figure that one out, I've just gotta find a girlfriend who would hold my legs up in the club. I don't know.'

Harry Shum Jr.

Harry Shum Jr. plays jock and Glee club member, Mike Chang. Before being cast as Mike, he had been in several dance-based movies. For his audition he combined some of the skills he had picked up from doing musicals when he first started acting. He really impressed everyone with his singing and dancing skills. Even though a show like *Glee* had never been done before, Harry knew it was going to be great and he really wanted to be part of it.

Even though Harry looks like he's always been a dancer, he hasn't. In high school, he had other interests and didn't even consider taking up dancing until his mates dared him to try out for the school dance team. Harry might have told them no, but he says the good-looking girls in the team made him think that it might be a good idea. He did so well in his try out that he made the team and the rest is history. If his mates hadn't dared him, he could be doing a boring office job by now or something equally dull; they really did him a massive favour that day.

Harry might have been to many auditions in the past but he still found his *Glee* audition really nerve-wracking. The worst part was waiting to see whether he had landed the part, but he forgot all about that once he got the nod. When he found out that he would be playing Mike, he did a little 'dance of excitement'.

Working on *Glee* has meant that Harry has had to sacrifice some of the things he used to like to do because he simply doesn't have the time anymore. He would love to be able to hit the gym and work out, but he can't – the rehearsals and filming of *Glee* are so physically

HARRY SHUM JR. IS AN
AMAZING DANCER.

draining that when he has a spare minute he likes to play video games instead.

Harry is Chinese, but he was born in Limon, Costa Rica. His Chinese parents set up a business there, but once Harry was a few years old they decided to move to America. Because of all the travelling that Harry has done, his first language is Spanish. He says that moving to America and having to learn English and Chinese messed him up at first – his mum and dad combined all three languages when they spoke so it must have been very confusing for a young Harry to figure out which bit was which language! It must have been tricky going to a new school, too.

As well as playing Mike in *Glee*, Harry also appears in the iPod adverts in the USA. He's doing another movie called *Step Up 3-D* and he belongs to LXD dance crew, which is a group of dancers who tell stories in dance. They performed on *So You Think You Can Dance* and any *Glee* fans that happened to miss it should check out some of the LXD videos on YouTube – they are amazing.

Harry has also danced with Mariah Carey, Beyoncé, Jessica Simpson and Jennifer Lopez which shows how much in demand as a dancer he is.

Asked by *Interview* magazine who he has enjoyed working with the most, Harry replied: 'My favourite artist and it's because we went on a tour called the

"Ladies First" tour and I was dancing for Beyoncé, and they had Missy Elliott, and Alicia Keys, and the best part of it – other than being on stage and dancing in front of thousands of people – was to actually every night go outside in the audience wherever I wanted and listen to Alicia Keys just do her thing. And you know, to me I felt like that was my soundtrack every day and I felt so lucky to be a part of that.'

If you are a big Harry fan, you should check him out on Twitter.

Heather Morris

Cheerios cheerleader Brittany in *Glee* is played by Heather Morris – she grew up in Arizona and started dancing when she was only one year old! Since then she hasn't stopped. Her passion in life is to dance and she made the big move to Los Angeles in 2006 to pursue her dream.

Like Amber, who auditioned for *American Idol*, Heather also auditioned for *So You Think You Can Dance*. She got through the first few rounds and made a great friend in Ben Susak. Both wanted so much to make it through to the live shows. Ben got a yes from the judges, but Heather got a no. She was gutted and couldn't help but burst into tears as soon as she left the stage. Many dancers might have given up, but Heather refused to do so. She was determined to keep on

HEATHER MORRIS DANCED
WITH BEYONCÉ ON HER
'SINGLE LADIES' TOUR.

dancing even if it meant watching the rest of *So You Think You Can Dance* from her sofa and trying something else instead.

Two years later Heather appeared in the American TV series *Swingtown*, a drama set in the 1970s. It wasn't a big hit and only 13 episodes were ever made. Heather was only in one episode so it can't have been that much of a disappointment when it was cancelled. She played a disco dancer in the episode 'Get Down Tonight', but she wasn't even on the credits.

After *Swingtown* she played another dancer in an episode of *Eli Stone*. This show was a comedy drama that starred Jonny Lee Miller in the lead role as an attorney who has hallucinations and does extraordinary things.

In 2009, Heather got her first acting break, playing Fiona in *Fired Up!* This movie was about two jocks from a football team who decide to swap football camp for cheerleader camp to meet girls. Heather's character Fiona was one of the cheerleaders.

Her next role was playing Brittany in *Glee* but unlike the rest of the cast, she didn't have an audition. In fact, she didn't think she would be appearing in *Glee* at all. She had been working as a support dancer for Beyoncé Knowles on her 2008 tour, The Beyoncé Experience, and appeared alongside Beyoncé when she performed at the American Music Awards. Heather was asked along to help teach Chris Colfer and the rest of the *Glee* actors how to dance to Beyoncé's 'Single Ladies'. Everyone was so impressed that they asked her to take on the role of the third cheerleader, even though she was seven years older than the character she was supposed to be playing.

Heather has turned what might have been a boring background character into one of the most entertaining ones. Everyone is looking forward to the funny things Brittany will say in the second season of *Glee*!

'Hell-O' – Season 1, Episode 14

The fourteenth episode of *Glee* is called 'Hell-O': it premièred in the USA on 3 April 2010 and first hit the UK screens on 19 April 2010.

In this episode, Sue Sylvester returns to the school after blackmailing Principal Figgins with an incriminating photograph of the two of them in bed together. She knows nothing went on, but he doesn't. Finn and Rachel's relationship isn't going well as Rachel is far too clingy and Finn can't stop thinking about Quinn. Sue realises that if she splits up Finn and Rachel then she might also cause New Directions to break up and so she tells Santana and Brittany that they have to seduce Finn. But it's all getting too much for Finn and he dumps Rachel, who is heartbroken. Finn foolishly goes on a date with Santana and Brittany and subsequently realises that Rachel is the girl he wants.

JONATHAN GROFF
PLAYS JESSE ST JAMES,
THE LEAD SINGER OF
NEW DIRECTIONS'
ARCH ENEMIES, VOCAL
ADRENALINE. THE
EPISODE 'HELL-O'
INTRODUCED JESSE AS
A PERMANENT
CHARACTER.

Meanwhile, while moping about in the library Rachel bumps into Jesse St. James, the lead singer of Vocal Adrenaline. They end up doing a duet performance of Lionel Richie's 'Hello' and Rachel quickly becomes smitten.

Rachel's new romance causes friction with the other members of New Directions when they find out and she is told that there is no way that she can date Jesse. They think he's only interested in her because it might help him to beat them at Regionals. Although Rachel promises she won't date him, she carries on and Jesse is more than happy to keep it a secret. Meanwhile, Finn is shocked when he asks Rachel if she'll date him again but she says no.

Emma and Will's relationship is stalling as Emma's obsession with cleanliness means that she doesn't feel comfortable kissing Will. She confesses that she is still a virgin and Will agrees to take it slow; he wants her to feel relaxed around him.

A few nights later Emma decides to cook a nice romantic meal for Will but her plans are ruined when his wife Terri lets herself into the apartment. Emma tells Terri that Will sang 'Hello Again' to her, but is devastated when Terri in turn reveals that the two of them danced to the same song at their high-school prom.

Will eventually betrays Emma when he visits Carmel

High to take a sneak peak at what Vocal Adrenaline are up to and ends up taking their coach Shelby Corcoran back to his apartment. They kiss passionately and almost sleep together before Will realises what he is doing and stops. Instead, he tells Shelby all about Emma and her problems in letting him close and she offers him some advice before she leaves.

The next day Emma shows Will his high-school yearbook, which proves that Terri was right about the importance of 'Hello Again'. Although Will is sorry that Emma is upset, for the time being they decide to split.

This episode introduces two new permanent characters – Shelby Corcoran, played by Idina Menzel, and Jesse St. James (Jonathan Groff). The cast perform covers of 'Hello, I Love You' by The Doors, The Beatles' 'Hello, Goodbye', 'Hello' by Lionel Richie, Neil Diamond's 'Hello Again', 'Highway to Hell' by AC/DC and 'Gives You Hell' by All-American Rejects.

SET SECRETS

In real life, Lea Michele and Jonathan Groff are best friends and so they were thrilled when they found out they'd be playing boyfriend and girlfriend on *Glee*. Matthew Morrison admitted to Fox that he found kissing Idina weird because he didn't know her very well, although he did know her husband. She hurt her chin because of Will's stubble, too. Ouch!

High School Musical

The *Glee* cast might hate it but people who have never seen the show always compare it to the *High School Musical* movies. They see lots of high-school kids singing and jump to conclusions, thinking that *Glee* is just for kids and teenagers. But *Glee* isn't like that at all: it deals with deep issues and adults of all ages love it and can't help but tune in each week.

Cory Monteith told the *Los Angeles Times*: 'I've heard it put like, "This is like *High School Musical*, if it's been punched in the stomach and had its lunch money stolen." People aren't singing the storylines, there's time to speak and there's time to sing.'

There's no way that *Glee* could be *High School Musical, the TV show* – creator Ryan Murphy has never seen any of the *High School Musical* movies and

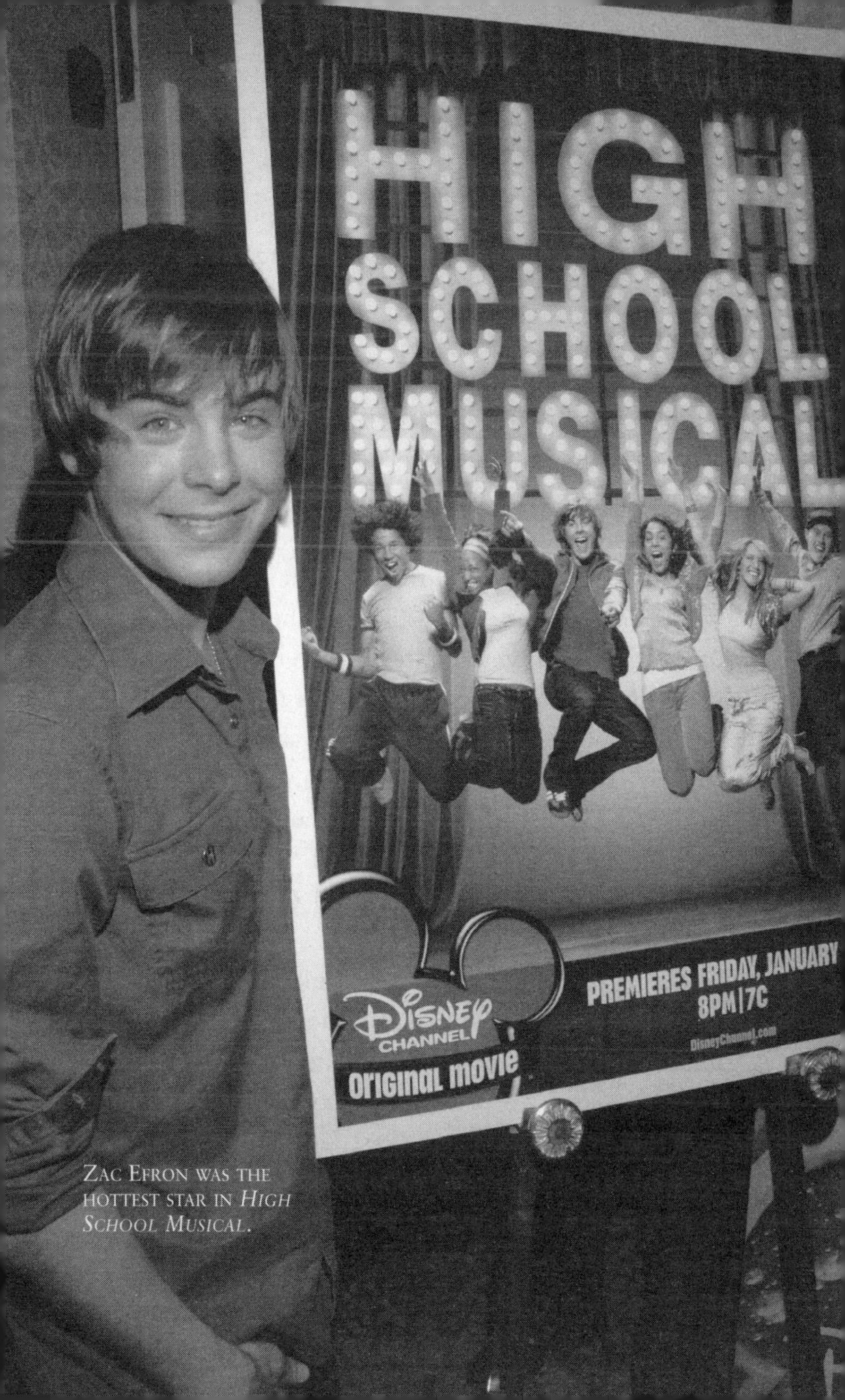

Zac Efron was the hottest star in *High School Musical*.

he wouldn't have wanted Finn and Rachel to burst into songs about school dinners and pencil cases. He wanted *Glee* to be a 'postmodern musical' and with the other two *Glee* creators, he was able to achieve this perfectly.

'Home' – Season 1, Episode 16

The sixteenth episode of *Glee* is called 'Home': it premièred in the USA on 27 April 2010 and first hit the UK screens on 3 May 2010.

In this episode Sue is thrilled that *Splits Magazine* want to do a piece on her and the Cheerios, but in her quest to make a great impression on the journalist she orders Mercedes to lose ten pounds in a week or face being dropped from the Cheerios – she doesn't want a chubby cheerleader on her team. She also forces Principal Figgins to lend her the auditorium so that she can put in extra practices, which leaves Will and New Directions in desperate need of somewhere else to rehearse.

Will heads to the local roller rink to see if they can hire it, only to bump into April Rhodes. She explains to him that she runs the place – she is the mistress of the wealthy tycoon who owns it. The two of them catch up on what's happened in the last few months and after Will tells her that he's looking to sublet his apartment, April confesses that she's looking for somewhere else to live. She forces Will to take her straight back to his place and ends up sleeping on the sofa until she climbs into bed next to him. The next morning Will tells her that she has to leave and that she deserves more than just being someone's mistress.

Mercedes stops eating as much but ends up hallucinating as she tries to lose weight. Her disappointing mid-week weigh-in shows that she has actually gained two pounds and so she tries anything and everything to get slimmer before Sue's deadline. Quinn sees what is happening and tells Mercedes that she's beautiful just the way she is and shouldn't have to change. A few days later, as the Cheerios get ready to perform for the journalist from *Splits Magazine* and the whole school, Mercedes decides to change what she's singing. She performs the Christina Aguilera classic 'Beautiful' and although Sue is at first angry, she soon calms down when the journalist commends her for arranging the wonderful performance and the message behind it. He promises to write a fantastic article praising Sue and her squad.

Also in this episode it is revealed that Kurt has set up his dad Burt with Finn's mother Carole because he thinks it will bring him and Finn closer together. He couldn't be more wrong, however, as Finn is devastated that his mother is moving on and selling some of his father's possessions. When he finally gets to meet Burt over a meal he realises that he's not so bad and they chat about their shared love of football; in contrast, Kurt is left feeling the odd one out and begins to think that his dad has more in common with Finn. He decides to get Finn to help him try and split their parents up, but Finn later decides that he can't do this because his mother is so happy and Burt has vowed never to hurt her.

Meanwhile, Will is surprised when he meets the 'new' April. She tells him that when she tried to tell the tycoon that she wouldn't be his mistress any more he had a stroke and died. The man's wife paid April $2 million to keep quiet about their affair and April has decided to share some of her newfound wealth with the Glee Club and buys the auditorium for them. She tells Will that she's off to Broadway to try and make her own dreams come true by launching the first all-white production of *The Wiz*.

This episode features covers of five songs: 'Beautiful' by Christina Aguilera, Dionne Warwick's 'A House Is Not a Home', a mash-up of Barbra Streisand's version of 'A House Is Not a Home' and 'One Less Bell to Answer', 'Fire' by The Pointer Sisters and 'Home' from *The Wiz*.

Apart from 'Fire', all these covers were released as singles and included on the album *Glee: The Music, Volume 3: Showstoppers*.

I is for...

Ian Brennan

Writer, producer and actor Ian Brennan is one of *Glee*'s three creators. Unlike his *Glee* characters, Ian didn't really enjoy singing when he was in high school but he did love acting and felt he had to join the choir to improve his chances of getting a part in his school's musical productions.

It was actually his theatre director at school who encouraged Ian to act and in many ways made him the great actor and writer he is today. He thought John Marquette was so great that he decided to make *Glee*'s director Will Schuester share many of his characteristics. His experiences of being in the school choir made him

IAN BRENNAN
THOUGHT MAKING A
SHOW ABOUT GLEE
CLUBS WOULD DO
REALLY WELL — HE
WAS RIGHT!

think that a movie on the subject would be a fantastic idea and so after he finished uni and was acting in Chicago and New York, he decided to start writing a screenplay. He told the *Daily Herald*: 'So I bought *Screenwriting for Dummies*, loaded screenwriting software into my computer and wrote a script. I figured if I didn't write it, someone else would, and then I'd always be kicking myself.'

Ian finished writing his first *Glee* script in 2005, but finding someone who could get it made proved a problem. For two years or so he tried to get his work to the right person, but he just kept getting no's. It wasn't until one of his friends passed it to *Nip/Tuck*'s Ryan Murphy that he received a positive reaction.

Reading the first *Glee* script excited Ryan but he didn't think it worked as a movie. He thought it would be better as a TV series and set about rewriting it with Ian and his friend Brad Falchuk. For Ian, the past few years have been a real whirlwind: 'It's been so weird. I was very happy doing my thing as an actor in New York, and then out of nowhere all this happens and I'm suddenly living in LA as a writer. I almost feel like this has all been an elaborate prank.'

Idina Menzel

Shelby Corcoran in *Glee* is played by Idina Menzel. Fans of the show actually suggested to the *Glee* creators that she should appear as Rachel's birth mother because she bears an uncanny resemblance to Lea Michele. Idina is a great actress, but she also writes her own songs and sings, too. She is best known for playing Maureen in the musical, *Rent*, and appeared as Elphaba in *Wicked*.

Like her fellow actress Lea Michele, Idina was born and raised in New York, and she loves the Big Apple. At fifteen years old, she got her first paid singing job singing at weddings and

IDINA MENZEL WITH HER HUSBAND TAYE DIGGS AT THE GLEE SPRING PREMIERE EPISODE OUTDOOR SCREENING.

Bar Mitzvahs – she must have enjoyed herself because she kept on singing at these events even when she was studying for a drama degree at New York University's Tisch School of the Arts.

On graduation, Idina secured that part of Maureen in the Broadway production of *Rent*. She did so well that she picked up a Tony nomination for Best Featured

Actress in a Musical. Following this, she decided to release a solo album: *Still I Can't Be Still*.

Idina has appeared in so many Broadway shows and plays, but it was playing Elphaba in *Wicked* that transformed her into a huge star. Fellow *Glee* actress Kristin Chenoweth was also in the original cast. In fact, Idina played the part twice – the second time around, she was earning $30,000 per week which shows just how big a star she had become.

Idina has been in lots of films too, including *Ask the Dust*, *Enchanted* and a movie version of *Rent*. She has also toured and performed her own music in so many different locations and still enjoys performing in New York whenever she can. In 2004, she released her second album, *Here*, and has sung on the *Beowulf* soundtrack. She also performed a duet with *X-Factor* runner-up Rhydian Roberts and he included 'What If' on his own album. In 2008, she released her third and most successful album to date: *I Stand*. The same year, she also released a charity single – 'Hope' – to raise money for Stand Up 2 Cancer.

Idina was really happy to be given the opportunity to play Shelby in *Glee*. She first appeared in the episode 'Hell-O', but it was five episodes later when it was revealed that she was Rachel's birth mother. In the final episode of Season 1, Shelby adopts Quinn's baby, but we'll have to wait and see how she adapts to looking after the child in Season 2.

Iqbal Theba

In *Glee*, Iqbal Theba plays Principal Figgins. He is a very experienced actor who has been in over 70 different films and TV shows. His first job was playing a citizenship student in the 1993 Robert Redford and Demi Moore movie, *Indecent Proposal*.

Iqbal loves working on *Glee*: he thinks the cast are great people (and great actors, too). He explained to *Starry Constellation* magazine why he believes the chemistry on set is so credible: 'First of all, I think the credit has to go to casting. Robert Ulrich, the casting director – that guy is amazing and a genius. He's cast me in, I don't know how many things before *Glee* so we go way back. I think the genius of Ryan Murphy and the casting director, they audition people and then they put them in the show and everything clicks, that doesn't really happen. I cannot imagine a character that doesn't really gel with everything and everybody else around them on the show – I think that's one part and the other part is the actors.

'Everyone is so wonderful, I'm amazed, and of course Jane is amazing and so is Jessalyn, Lea, and Matthew. There are people who had never really worked in television or theater like Chris Colfer, and that guy amazes me – I think he's like nineteen years old. Some of these youngsters are just amazing: they are such wonderful actors, they're triple threats. They

IQBAL THEBA HAS HAD GREAT FUN PLAYING PRINCIPAL FIGGINS.

can sing, they can dance, they can act and a lot of credit goes to the entire cast with making it work with their own characters and the other actors, whatever they're creating.'

Iqbal thinks it's strange that he gets lots of people coming up to him to ask for autographs and photos because he plays such a minor part in *Glee*. Cory Monteith and Lea Michele might be the biggest stars, but every member of the *Glee* cast has a huge fan base, it seems.

J is for...

Jacob Ben Israel (Played By Josh Sussman)

The biggest nerd on *Glee* is Jacob Ben Israel and although he isn't a member of the Glee club, he is obsessed with Rachel Berry and constantly tries to persuade her to go out with him. He is really creepy and his behaviour would freak anyone out. The way he talks to Rachel and demands that she lets him have some of her underwear or touch her bra is horrible.

Jacob wears glasses and has an Afro. He knows all the gossip on everyone at William McKinley High School and is the editor of the school newspaper. Jacob can be quite spiteful and isn't afraid to blackmail people to get what he wants.

The actor who plays him, Josh Sussman, loves playing such an oddball character.

Jane Lynch

Cheerios head coach Sue Sylvester is played by Jane Lynch. She was a great actress to get on board because of her vast experience and her acting skills are simply the best when it comes to comedy. Sue is one busy lady and so at first it was thought that she would just have a recurring role in *Glee* but when another project fell through, she was able to play Sue the whole time.

JOSH SUSSMAN

Her extensive film résumé includes *Julie & Julia*, *Post Grad*, *For Your Consideration*, *A Mighty Wind*, *Best in Show* and *Lemony Snicket's A Series of Unfortunate Events*. Jane has also appeared in several TV shows, including *Lovespring International*, *Desperate Housewives*, *Criminal Minds*, *Boston Legal*, *Two and a Half Men* and *The New Adventures of Old Christine*.

JANE LYNCH
LOOKING
GORGEOUS IN
OLIVE GREEN AT
THE GOLDEN
GLOBE AWARDS.

All in all, she has acted in over 130 different films and TV shows. Wow!

Over the years, Jane has played some really interesting characters but Sue must be one of her favourites. She told TV.com: 'I always say when I put on that tracksuit I have a license to say anything I want. I think it's probably very good therapy because I'm a much nicer person at home. I get it all out at work, and that kind of contemptuousness and heinous behavior is just very shallowly below the surface for me, so it's kind of nice.'

Unlike her fellow *Glee* actors, dancing has never been one of Jane's great loves. To get her dancing skills up to scratch, she has had to put in so much effort. Doing her musical number was harder than she thought it might be because even though she loves to sing, she wasn't as good at it as she had imagined she would be and freely admits that the *Glee* choreographer Zach Woodlee had to help her out a few times.

Although Jane is happy playing Sue, she would still like the opportunity to stand on the other side of the camera and direct. Hopefully she will get to do a bit of directing on *Glee* – no doubt she would make a great director. She admits: 'I think I'd like to. I haven't spoken to anybody about it, but I love directing and I love calling the shots. I think [*Glee*] would be a great place to do it, because the directors we get and the writers we have are just so amazing. Our DP [director of photography Chris Baffa] is great, because you have to have a great DP, if you want to be a great director. I think I'm learning at the feet of many masters.'

Like *Glee* creator Ian Brennan, who based the part of Will on one of his old teachers, Jane modelled Sue on a real person. She had an acting teacher at college who was nicknamed 'the dragon lady' and was the Sue character in Jane's life. The dragon lady scared her students and made them feel useless before

JANE LYNCH WITH MERYL STREEP IN *JULIE & JULIA*.

'building them up'. Naturally, her classes were not much fun at all. Jane did well to stick with the acting as some people might have quit if their teacher was like that.

Jayma Mays

Guidance counsellor Emma Pillsbury in *Glee* is played by Jayma Mays. Unlike Lea Michele and Matthew Morrison she has never been on Broadway, but she did appear in several high-profile TV series before getting the part of Emma.

Jayma went to Radford University and graduated with a degree in Performing Arts. She started her TV career in 2004 when she appeared in the *Friends*' spin-off show *Joey* alongside Matt LeBlanc. Since then she has not stopped. She played Charlie in *Ugly Betty*, Elsa in *Pushing Daisies* and another character called Charlie in *Heroes*, as well as other small parts in numerous TV shows.

In addition to TV shows, Jayma has been in several movies, including Wes Craven's *Red Eye* and Clint Eastwood's *Flags of Our Fathers*. She played Kevin James' character's love interest in *Paul Blart: Mall Cop*, too.

Jayma knew she wanted to play Emma before she had even read a full *Glee* script. Although she had only seen a few sides from the pilot episode, she recognised

JAYMA WITH HER HUSBAND
ADAM CAMPBELL.

instantly that Emma was the perfect role for her. She told The TV Chick: 'There was so much going on with her just from those few sheets of paper that I had, kind of describing who she was. I knew immediately that there was a lot that was going to be going on with her and I think that's hard to find sometimes with roles for women: there's maybe not so many layers to them, always. And I just felt from the get go that there was so much going on. And I also knew that Ryan Murphy was involved. I knew that was exciting to me, too. As soon as I heard that, I knew that there would be something good on the page, so I was immediately drawn to it.'

Playing Emma has been great for Jayma but the only downside is that she has become a tiny bit obsessive about cleaning her hands. She explained: 'After the first few weeks, after we got picked up and we started filming the first few episodes, I kind of started getting that feeling of needing to wash my hands all the time. And I started keeping anti-bacterial stuff in my purse, just because you start thinking about that stuff more, just naturally, because they're kinda shoving it in your face at work all the time. I'm not wearing rubber gloves at home, but I definitely keep a little Purell [hand sanitiser] in my pocketbook now.'

Now that's really funny!

Many *Glee* fans think that Jayma is the luckiest

woman in the world because she got to kiss Matthew Morrison who plays Will in the episode 'Sectionals'. Kissing Matthew was relatively painless for Jayma because she knows him pretty well and they had done lots of episodes prior to their romantic scenes; she had also worked with him on another project. She might have found it harder if she had had to kiss him in the first episode, for instance. Jayma thinks it really helps if you know your onscreen love interest because it makes you feel comfortable.

Even though their characters are supposed to be enemies, Jayma also loves working with Jessalyn Gilsig (who plays Will's wife, Terri) on the show and they get on like a house on fire. Jessalyn is probably Jayma's best friend on set because they always have a good time hanging out and this makes filming their scenes really enjoyable too, even though they are mean to each other.

Unlike the majority of the cast who have all performed on Broadway, Jayma has never been that much of a singer and she found filming her musical number 'I Could Have Danced All Night' for the 'Mash-Up' episode pretty daunting. She was so nervous before takes that she had to 'keep eating bread and toast because my stomach was so sick.' She also messed up the dance routine a bit because she kept stepping on Matthew Morrison's feet. Jayma might not think she did amazingly well, but the version we saw on our TV screens looked perfect and caused many fans to shed a tear.

Working on *Glee* has encouraged all the cast members to think back to when they were at school. Jayma was quite busy then and was in lots of different groups rather than just one group. She liked being a member of the cheerleaders' squad, monologue club and math club, so she didn't really define herself, unlike so many other students.

When The TV Chick asked her which character in the Glee club she can relate to best, she replied: 'I can kind of identify with all of them a little bit. I wasn't a Rachel character, but I definitely had ambition. I think she's the extreme of what ambitious kids might feel like. And I feel like there are kind of extremes with a few of the kids. I guess I had ambition, I knew I wanted to do something different – I didn't know if it was possible at the time, but I knew that I kind of had that drive. But also, I did want to try and fit in with some of the kids at school, like being a cheerleader is all about trying to fit in a little and be a part of that world, so I think I probably identify with a few of them, but not one in particular.'

Jenna Ushkowitz

Glee's shy Tina Cohen-Chang is played by Jenna Ushkowitz – she might only be in her early twenties, but she has already been in the Broadway productions of *The King and I* and *Spring Awakening*. She was actually working with Lea Michele in *Spring Awakening* when she was spotted and asked to audition for *Glee*.

Jenna has always loved acting and singing, and first appeared on TV shows when she was three years old. She was on *Sesame Street*, *Reading Rainbow* and *As the World Turns*. In addition to this, she has acted in the independent films *Babyface* and *Educated*, and presented a sports show called *Yankees on Deck*.

Jenna grew up in East Meadow, Long Island, New York and still lives in New York today. When she's filming *Glee* she has to live in Los Angeles, but the Big Apple will always be her home and she is constantly going back and forth.

She has said: 'I'm hoping that I can be bi-coastal and have the best of both worlds. I think I'll always relate NY with theatre and LA to TV/Film land. New York will always be home for me and I love the city more than anything; I'll always have a special place for NY in my heart and I find myself travelling back to NY whenever I can to visit family and friends and just be with the energy the city brings! (I'm on the plane right now – headed back to LA from a short visit

glee

JENNA LOOKS SO
CUTE AT THE
GLEE PREMIÈRE!

FOX

in NY!) LA is a new place for me and I'm slowly building a life there that I am enjoying very, very much. It's a much chiller vibe and I love having a car to get places in LA. I don't think I can compare them, I love them both!'

Jenna might love New York but she was actually born in Seoul, which is the largest city in South Korea. She moved to New York when she was adopted. She was only three months old. Unlike her *Glee* co-star Cory Monteith, Jenna enjoyed school and was a member of the Glee club. She also made sure she graduated before becoming a full-time actress on Broadway.

Jenna can't decide which member of the *Glee* cast she likes the most because they are all so close. She told Gleefan.com: 'We are all such a tight-knit family and we all love each other so much, it's kind of amazing and rare. We all have a really special bond and I'm very appreciative of every cast/crew member we have. Most of us spend a lot of time with each other off-screen too, which creates an amazing chemistry that I think definitely reads during our scenes.'

Jenna enjoys watching films and listening to music. Her favourite actors who have inspired her are Kate Winslet, Leonardo DiCaprio, Sandra Oh, Johnny Depp and Sean Penn. They have all enjoyed long acting careers and been in lots of different types of movie: drama, comedy, action, animated and rom-coms. Jenna's fans would love it if she had such a varied movie career and picked up an Oscar or two.

Although Jenna loves working on *Glee*, it seems her heart belongs to Broadway. She explained to Gleefan.com: 'I have to say, as a theatre trained actor, there is nothing like Broadway/live theatre. I love the instant response and energy from the audience. TV is a completely different world and I'm pretty new to it, so I'm enjoying learning new things everyday – but *Glee* is the ultimate dream because we get to do both!'

Jenna loves the *Glee* musical numbers and told PopSugar: '"Somebody to Love" was probably my favourite just because we finally felt like we were bonded, like a real Glee club. Just personally, I think that "Single Ladies" was really fun.'

The whole cast had to learn to dance and sing as a unit, which was quite a challenge. One *Glee* fan asked Jenna if it was difficult to learn to sing as a choir. She answered: 'I think that just like the dancing, we are definitely learning about our fellow *Glee* members and are learning how we sound as a unit and how we move. It's always going to be difficult at first when you are melding and blending – but it's been such an enjoyable experience with all the talent that I think we enjoy the challenge – resulting in a very rewarding feeling when we work together.'

JENNA AND KEVIN MCHALE ARE REALLY GOOD FRIENDS OUTSIDE OF WORK TOO.

Jessalyn Gilsig

Will's wife on *Glee* (Terri Schuester) is played by Jessalyn Gilsig and she is a highly experienced actress who has appeared on *Boston Public*, *Prison Break*, *CSI: NY* and *Heroes*. She played the obsessive Gina Russo in *Nip/Tuck* and so she already knew *Glee* creators Brad Falchuk and Ryan Murphy because they were writers on that TV show, too. Because she knew them really well, she was convinced that *Glee* was going to be great.

She explained to HitFix: 'Having worked with Ryan before, I had so much confidence in him creatively. I knew he had a vision, I just knew it. There are no accidents in Ryan's world, or if there are accidents, they're accidents you can capitalize on. So for me, coming from that advantage of having watched him develop characters on *Nip/Tuck*, I have a very genuine trust that he is watching and conscious, and that things that you're watching and saying, "What? Where is this going?", he's on top of it as well. In that sense, I was up for it from the moment I read the script.'

Jessalyn was born in Canada and started acting when she was twelve years old. She is married to film producer Bobby Salomon and they have one daughter.

She was thrilled to get the opportunity to play Terri in *Glee*. Working on the show has made her think about what she would do if she could turn back the

JESSALYN IS REALLY ENJOYING GETTING TO WORK WITH RYAN MURPHY AGAIN.

clock and do high school again. She told one interviewer she would change: 'Everything, I would relax a little more. I thought everybody knew what was going on except me, and that I was completely missing the boat. Now I think I was probably on par with everybody else. So, I'd just cut myself some slack and have more fun.'

Jessalyn's acting career started properly in 1995 when she moved to New York and appeared in several plays. She moved into television a few years later, with roles in action-adventure TV series, *Viper* and time-travel TV series, *Seven Days*.

Jessalyn has been in movies too. Her biggest roles were playing Lucy in *The Horse Whisperer* with Robert Redford, Callie in *A Cooler Climate* alongside Sally Field and Robert Carlyle's onscreen wife Sam in the 2007 movie *Flood*.

Jessalyn is a keen artist and when she's not busy filming *Glee* or one of her other TV shows, she likes to paint. She is very talented and one of her paintings appeared in the movie, *The Station Agent*.

Jesse St. James (played by Jonathan Groff)

Rachel Berry might get her heart broken by Finn when he dumps her, but she soon gets over him when she bumps into Jesse St. James in the library. Jesse is the male lead of Vocal Adrenaline and so Rachel should hate him but somehow she can't – she's thrilled to have met someone who's just as good at singing as she is. New Directions might tell Rachel that she can't date Jesse but after he transfers to McKinley High, they can't do anything about it. Rachel is falling for him and a devious Jesse is thrilled. After a few weeks Jesse suggests that they should have sex and after much thought, Rachel decides that she is ready to do so. At the last minute she backs out, though, and the two decide to wait.

The other members of New Directions might think that Jesse is a spy, but we soon learn that he has a more important agenda: he has to try and encourage Rachel to search for her long-lost birth mother so she can find out that it's actually Shelby, his Vocal Adrenaline coach. When Rachel was born, Shelby signed a contract to say that she wouldn't contact Rachel until she was eighteen and so Rachel has to be the one to find her mother, not the other way round. Jesse might be dating Rachel as a favour to Shelby but the longer he spends with her, the more he likes her. He leaves once Rachel realises that Shelby is her mother and goes back to Vocal Adrenaline with only days to go before Regionals.

So, is Jesse a good guy or a bad guy? We'll just have to wait and see in Season 2!

Jonathan Groff

Jonathan Groff plays Jesse St. James in *Glee*. He is a multi-talented singer-songwriter and actor who has appeared in numerous stage productions, TV shows and films.

Jonathan was born in Lancaster, Pennsylvania. He graduated from Conestoga Valley High School in 2003 and is best known for playing Melchior Gabor in the play *Spring Awakening*, though he has also played Rolf in a National Tour of *The Sound of Music* and performed in the musicals *Fame, Hair* and *In My Life*. In 2007, he was nominated for a Tony Award for Best Leading Actor. He has also been nominated for another four acting awards, winning two of them: a Theatre World Award in 2007 and an Obie Award in 2009.

In fact, Jonathan acted alongside Lea Michele in *Spring Awakening* on Broadway and so knew her long before he was cast in *Glee*. He was actually the one who introduced Lea to *Glee* creator Ryan Murphy: without his help, she might have never been cast.

Jonathan might be a successful actor now but he has had his fair share of part-time jobs in the past. He was a counsellor at an acting camp, waited tables and operated a ride in a kids' theme park. As well as acting on stage, he took on the role of Woodstock organiser Michael Lang in the film *Taking Woodstock* and

JONATHAN GROFF AND LEA
MICHELE KNEW EACH OTHER PRE-
GLEE, HAVING APPEARED TOGETHER
IN *SPRING AWAKENING*.

played Henry Mackler in the American soap, *One Life to Live*.

Since first appearing in *Glee* in the episode 'Hell-O', Jonathan hasn't stopped working and he has two films out in 2010: *The Conspirator* and *Twelve Thirty*.

Josh Sussman

Glee oddball Jacob Ben Israel is played by Josh Sussman: he was born in New York and has spent his whole life living there. For two years, he studied at the city's School for Film and Television to enable him to learn as much about acting as possible. He has had to move to LA to film *Glee*, though.

Jacob isn't the first big role that Josh has played. He has been acting in TV shows since 2005, but is probably most famous for playing Hugh Normous in the Disney children's series *Wizards of Waverly Place* alongside Selena Gomez and David Henrie.

If Josh wasn't such a great actor then the part of Jacob would probably have been quite forgettable and might not even feature in this *Glee A-Z*. He explained to Young Hollywood: 'Originally it was just supposed to be just one episode – just a jock in the celibacy club, and just a horny guy – and Ryan Murphy was just so generous, and he expanded the part and gave me so much more to do. The name was originally Randy Henkiss and they changed it to Jacob

QUIRKY JOSH SUSSMAN
HAS LOADS OF HAIR!

Ben Israel, it's a little cooler. I guess they liked what I did, Ryan had vision and he just said, "I want to bring you back for another one," and then he let me be a Rachel Berry stalker.'

Jacob might be a big weirdo, but Josh thinks he's a great character to play. He describes him as 'creepy endearing'. Josh really enjoys filming his scenes with Lea Michele. When he was asked by one interviewer what the chemistry is like with Rachel, he replied: 'It's really cool, like I think, yeah one time before when we're just getting into character, before take I say, "Lea, you've got something in your eye" and she's like, [touching her eye] I was like, "Never mind, it's just a sparkle."'

He is such a joker in interviews and likes saying that he loves Lea Michele and blowing kisses down cameras for her. Josh might enjoy playing a stalker, but when the shoe is on the other foot, he feels a bit freaked out: he has had lots of people add him on Facebook and send him flattering messages, but sometimes they are a bit over-the-top. He has to be careful with the replies that he gives because some fans lie about their age and he could land himself in big trouble.

High school wasn't the happiest place for Josh when he was growing up, so working on *Glee* has probably dragged up some bad memories that he would rather forget. He wasn't Mr Popular and did get bullied quite a bit; he enjoyed being in the drama club and the chess club too, even though he was shy and a bit of a loner. Some of the people who bullied him have recently got in touch: now that he's famous they want to be his friend and have apologised for past behaviour. Josh isn't taken in, though – he's not interested in spending time with people who treated him so badly in the past.

He told Young Hollywood the message he wants to give to the bullies: 'This is the revenge: yeah, are you sorry you bullied me, right? Wish you didn't push me into that locker, huh? What you doing now? Pumping gas? That was kinda mean, I shouldn't have. They write to me and they're like, "I'm sorry I was mean to you in high school. So you're doing well now – when you're back in Jersey, we should get together."'

In the second season of *Glee* Josh hopes that Rachel will decide to get Finn jealous by kissing Jacob. It sounds unlikely, but you never know with *Glee*!

'Journey' – Season 1, Episode 22

The twenty-second episode of *Glee* and the first season finale is called 'Journey': it premièred in the USA on 8 June 2010 and first hit the UK screens on 14 June 2010.

In this episode the judges for Regionals are announced and Will can't believe Sue is one of them.

New Directions are gutted because they think Sue will do her best to make sure they lose. The other judges are Josh Groban, Olivia Newton-John and news anchor Rod Remington.

Will goes to Emma for advice but instead ends up feeling far worse when she reveals that she's dating her dentist. Finn tries to make Rachel smile again and feel more confident about their chances at Regionals and she kisses him.

At Regionals we get to meet Aural Intensity, the other glee club competing with New Directions and Vocal Adrenaline for the title of Best Glee Club. Aural Intensity perform first and do a mash-up of Josh Groban's 'You Raise Me Up' and Olivia Newton-John's 'Magic'. New Directions start to feel under more pressure and Will is forced to give them a pep talk to convince them that they can compete with the others.

Just before they perform, Finn decides to tell Rachel that he loves her. They've chosen songs by Journey and do a great mash-up of 'Any Way You Want It' and 'Lovin' Touchin' Squeezin''. Their other numbers are the love song, 'Faithfully', and the classic anthem, 'Don't Stop Believin''

Quinn's mother Judy is in the audience and she tells her daughter that she can move back home – it seems her judgmental father won't be controlling them any more because Judy has kicked him out for having an affair. Seconds after Quinn gets the good news, her waters break and she is rushed to hospital. Meanwhile, Vocal Adrenaline chooses Queen's 'Bohemian Rhapsody' as one of their songs. After she gives birth Quinn asks Puck if he loved her. Puck tells her that he's always loved her, back then and now.

Rachel asks Shelby if she will teach at McKinley High but she turns the offer down – she wants to concentrate on starting a family. Shelby gets her wish of having a baby as she adopts Quinn's baby and names her Beth.

As the judges discuss the winner of Regionals it's clear that they have different favourites. Josh Groban proclaims that New Directions were the only group with heart, but the other judges don't agree. As the winners are announced everyone feels nervous: the whole future of New Directions depends on the result. Sue announces that Aural Intensity have come second and, after a dramatic pause, it is revealed that Vocal Adrenaline have won again, while New Directions finish in last place.

Emma tries her best to convince Principal Figgins to save New Directions but he won't listen. After being on and off for weeks, Will and Emma finally get back on track when Will tells her that he loves her and they kiss.

Sue is touched when she hears New Directions perform

Lulu's 'To Sir, with Love' for Will as a way of thanking him for all he has done for them. We then find out that Sue actually voted for New Directions to win Regionals but was outvoted by the other judges. She pays Principal Figgins a visit and blackmails him into letting them have another year of Glee Club. When Will finds out what she's done he can't believe it: never in a million years had he thought that his sworn enemy would save New Directions after trying to bring it down all year. To celebrate, he and the members of New Directions sing 'Over the Rainbow'.

In this episode the *Glee* cast sing covers of Queen's 'Bohemian Rhapsody', 'To Sir, with Love' by Lulu, Judy Garland's classic 'Over the Rainbow', a mash-up of Olivia Newton-John's 'Magic' and Josh Groban's 'You Raise Me Up', Journey's 'Faithfully', 'Don't Stop Believin'' and a mash-up of 'Any Way You Want It' and 'Lovin' Touchin' Squeezin''.

None of the covers were released as singles but all apart from the mash-up of 'Magic' and 'You Raise Me Up' were included on the album *Glee: The Music, Journey to Regionals*.

K is for...

Ken Tanaka (Played By Patrick Gallagher)

Ken Tanaka is the William McKinley High School football coach played by the Chinese-Irish actor, Patrick Gallagher.

Ken is a macho guy and so he isn't the biggest fan of the Glee club, but when Kurt proves that he can kick as well as dance, he is more than happy to welcome him onto the team. Even though he knows she has feelings for Will, he proposes to Emma and is determined to show her that he's the right guy for her. In the episode 'Sectionals', however, he dumps her at the altar when he realises that she will never love him enough.

Patrick loves putting on Ken's football uniform because it helps him get into character really easily. He knows that as soon as he puts on the short shorts and tight T-shirts that he is Ken, the Japanese football coach.

During an interview with *Starry Constellation Magazine* Patrick was asked what it is about playing Ken that he finds challenging. He replied: 'Part of it is walking around with those shorts and those socks, that's always a bit of a challenge! Ken is such an interesting character to me because I have to go to parts of my own insecurities – parts of my own, for lack of a better term, bitterness. So I think the challenge is to try and find that. I also probably play with the subtle humor that they write; the writing is so great that I think the real challenge is to find the balance between not trying to be too funny, not trying to make it funny, just letting it be funny, and just delivering the line and letting the writing do the work for you.'

Asked what/who he based Ken on, Patrick told them: 'I draw a lot of Ken from me: Ken is a lot more like me than I would like to admit. All actors, for every role, I think we try to find a part of ourselves but like I said, I draw from me. It's a bit of a challenge for me to go there and I kind of understand him in a lot of ways. You go to that part that relates to that character for the emotional part. For the coach part, we've all had football, baseball, and gym teachers so I think I am channeling a lot of my old high school teachers in the way that they operate as a coach.'

Kevin McHale

Texan Kevin McHale plays Artie Abrams in *Glee*. A supertalented singer and dancer, he was over the moon when he got cast as Artie. He must have done really well in his audition because Chris Colfer also went for the part, but didn't get it.

Kevin first got into performing after appearing in several local TV ads. His first TV role was playing a character called Mark in one episode of *All That*. He was only fifteen at the time, so it was a big deal to get a part in the sketch comedy/musical show. It was nearly two years later before he landed his next role: playing Neil in *Ruthless*.

Ruthless is a short film of less than seven minutes, which tells the story of two vicious young girls called Iris and Lex, who trick another girl into climbing a ladder onto a roof. As soon as she gets to the roof, they remove the ladder and run inside the house, leaving Ruth stranded. The poor girl looks so miserable and upset, but when she glances to her right, she sees her hunky neighbour Neil (played by Kevin) going for a swim. He asks her what she's doing and after he completes each lap in the swimming pool, he asks for her advice. The two horrible girls return and are livid when they hear Neil swimming up and down and talking to their victim. They put the ladder back up and order Ruth to come down, but she refuses – she is quite happy where she is.

THE 41ST NAACP
IMAGE
AWARDS

FOX

KEVIN MCHALE USED
TO BE IN A BOY BAND!

The leader, Lexi, asks Ruth if she is coming to play at her house the next day, but Ruth shrugs her shoulders and declares, 'I don't know yet,' then turns back in the direction of Neil.

This dark comedy is well worth a watch, so why not check it out on YouTube?

Shortly before Kevin shot *Ruthless*, he was signed up for a new boy band called NLT (Not Like Them). It was a really big achievement because it is hard to get a recording deal anywhere, let alone in the USA. Kevin was joined in the band by Travis Garland, Justin Joseph 'JJ' Thorne and Vahe 'V' Sevani. They made some great records, with cool dance moves as well as great vocals. Only a month after their first single 'That Girl' came out, they opened for the Pussycat Dolls. Wow! Kevin and the rest of the band must have felt like all their dreams were coming true.

Their song 'Heartburn' was picked to appear on the soundtrack for *Bratz: The Movie*, which brought them to the attention of millions of young girls worldwide. In August 2007, they released their second single, 'She Said, I Said (Time We Let Go)' and in the December they brought out their own take on the classic Christmas carol 'Silent Night'.

The year 2007 might have been great for NLT, but 2008 definitely wasn't. They took part in the 'Bandemonium' tour with Menudo, VFactory and

Glowb, but it didn't do as well as expected and their fourth single 'Karma' was to be their last. Their planned album *Not Like Them* was never released and they officially broke up in 2009.

Poor Kevin must have been gutted when his band split after showing so much promise at the start – they could have been as big as Backstreet Boys or Westlife.

Luckily Kevin had continued to act while being in the band and so he had something to fall back on. As well as playing the hunky neighbour in *Ruthless*, he was in the BBC comedy *The Office* and Jamie Lynn Spear's *Joey 101*. He then appeared in two episodes of *True Blood* (as a character called Neil Jones) before being cast in *Glee*.

Really, it is quite remarkable that Kevin wanted to continue with showbiz after NLT folded, when most people would have wanted the ground to swallow them up and headed home with their tails between their legs.

Kevin might have originally thought that being in a boy band was his perfect job but actually getting the part of Artie Abrams in *Glee* was even better at showcasing his many talents. He explained to journalist Jamie Steinberg why he wanted to be part of *Glee*: 'At first, it seemed too good to be true. There was no way that there'd be such a combination of singing, acting and getting to do these amazing songs in the midst of a crazy Ryan Murphy script. I read the pilot and laughed out loud the entire time. So, I just set my mind to doing anything and everything I could do to be a part of the show.'

His *Glee* audition didn't go to plan but it still impressed everyone who was there. Kevin told Backstage.com: 'I auditioned fairly early for Artie, and I thought I did awful. I sang "Let It Be" and I cut part of the song out 'cause I thought it was too boring, and then in the middle of the song, they're like, "Okay, keep singing, don't stop!" I was like, "I don't know any more words!" Everybody was laughing in the waiting room. But they asked me back, and then I had to wait six weeks to go test – I was a nervous wreck. We all tested together – Jenna [Tina] and Chris [Kurt] and I. And here we are.'

Playing Artie was a big challenge at first because Kevin had to get used to spending all his time in a wheelchair and having to keep his feet still during the musical numbers. Most of the *Glee* cast based their characters on teachers or people they knew in high school – Kevin didn't need to do this because he has always been a bit of an 'Artie.'

'I'm a complete nerd myself and I think I've always been drawn to those types in movies and on TV,' he confessed to *Starry Constellation Magazine*. 'So, I was really able to tap into that part of myself quite easily, but Artie is amazingly good-hearted. I'd say he is naive, in a good way, to a lot of the drama that goes on around him because all he really cares about is making sure the Glee club is always there and doing its best. I can completely relate to wanting to do something you're passionate about and the drive to keep that dream alive, whether it's wanting to sing in Glee club or for me wanting to act.'

From day one on set, he knew that he had done the right thing in signing up for *Glee*. It was completely different from anything he'd ever done before and a real blast to shoot. He even enjoyed getting thrown into the port-o-potty (portable toilet) in the pilot episode.

Kevin is really passionate about *Glee* and loves the fact that so many people get so much enjoyment from watching it every week. He says: 'The show is completely about the underdog and I think people naturally want to root for the underdog. Besides the fact that we're singing songs everyone knows, from classic rock to songs that are on the radio now, without being cliché, the show is like every good thing I've liked or seen, all rolled into one. It's positive, it's funny, it's witty and sometimes a bit cruel, but that's the best part – you never know what's coming next!'

Kissing

Doing kissing scenes can be nerve-wracking and strange for most actors and actresses because they have to kiss passionately someone that they have never kissed before. Even though the *Glee* cast are all great friends, they still found locking lips tough.

For Will and Emma's kissing scene in the 'Sectionals' episode, both Jayma Mays (who plays Emma) and Matthew Morrison (Will) felt under a lot of pressure. Jayma was the most nervous about it and brushed her teeth a couple of times before shooting started. Matthew was a lot more relaxed and munched on some peanut M&Ms. He joked to Jayma shortly before their kiss that he hadn't brushed his teeth at all that day. Poor Jayma!

Jayma might have been feeling nervous, but that didn't show on screen. They had to keep kissing each other for six or seven takes. It's a good job they are such good friends!

Lea Michele and Cory Monteith might have kissed a few times now because they play Rachel and Finn, but they haven't revealed to journalists what it was like to have to kiss each other. So far, they have kept how they feel about their kissing scenes a big secret, but they may spill the beans one day.

Season 2 of *Glee* will no doubt bring more kissing scenes so we'll just have to wait and see who kisses whom.

As well as kisses onscreen, the *Glee* cast has been attracting attention for their kisses off-screen. When Cory Monteith kissed *Hairspray* star Nikki Blonsky on the cheek at a Carol-oke, he never expected that this would be big news for gossip websites. He was wearing big reindeer antlers at the time and they were on stage too, so there was no way it could be interpreted as a romantic gesture.

He actually set the record straight about his feelings for Lea Michele at the same event. Cory announced: 'We're great friends. We've become really close over the show, but we're just friends: we're not dating.'

Kurt Hummel (Played By Chris Colfer)

The flamboyant Kurt Hummel is one of *Glee*'s most popular characters. He is played by Chris Colfer.

Kurt's heart lies in the Glee club and performing. He loves drama and dance as well as singing. At first he is an easy target for the football team because he is small in stature and effeminate so they bully him, but he later gains their respect when he proves that he can kick and help them win football games.

Kurt likes to look good and always makes sure that he is wearing the latest trends. He auditioned for New Directions in the pilot by singing 'Mr. Cellophane' from *Chicago*. This was actually the song that Chris sang in his first *Glee* audition, too.

Like all the members of the Glee club, Kurt has some identity problems as he tries to fit in. He wants his dad to be proud of him and so he joins the football team to prove that he can be the son his father wants. Later on

KURT HUMMEL, PLAYED BY CHRIS COLFER, IS ONE OF THE SHOW'S MOST POPULAR CHARACTERS.

in the episode 'Preggers', he admits to his dad that he is gay, only for his father to say that he has known for many years.

Kurt has a big crush on his fellow Glee club member Finn Hudson and hopes to offer him a shoulder to cry on if he ends his relationship with Quinn. He knows that Rachel has her eye on Finn and so he tries to stop anything from developing by giving her a bad makeover.

L is for...

'Laryngitis' – Season 1, Episode 18

The eighteenth episode of *Glee* is called 'Laryngitis': it premièred in the USA on 11 May 2010 and first hit the UK screens on 17 May 2010.

In this episode Puck realises that he has to do something after he's thrown into the trash for shaving off his mohawk by his former friends. He decides that he needs to date Mercedes because this will raise his social status as she has become very popular since joining the Cheerios. Mercedes starts off staying she won't date him, but after he performs 'The Lady is a Tramp' for her, she starts to think dating Puck wouldn't be so bad after all. Santana is offended that she has yet again been dismissed by Puck and has a sing-off with Mercedes to 'The Boy Is Mine' – Will has to step in to stop them coming to blows.

Later, when Mercedes sees Puck throwing people into the trash she realises that he's still the same bully and so she tells him it's over – no man of hers can do that. She also realises that her heart belongs to the Glee Club and subsequently resigns from the Cheerios.

Meanwhile, Rachel goes to Will with evidence that Finn, Puck, Quinn, Brittany and Santana are only faking that they are singing in rehearsals. She doesn't think it's at all fair and decides to sing 'The Climb' by Miley Cyrus. Instead of sounding great, her performance is pretty awful, though – it's clear to everyone that she is losing her voice. With Finn in tow, she goes to the doctor for support but is horrified when the doctor suggests she might need to have surgery: she is petrified because she thinks that surgery could permanently damage her voice, even though it's low-risk. However, she thinks that without her amazing singing voice, she'd be nothing. Finn knows that she's being melodramatic and takes her to visit his friend Sean. His former football buddy is now paralysed from the upper chest down, but still manages to keep smiling. Sean teaches Rachel that she has more than just a good voice. A few days later, she returns to his bedside to tell him that the antibiotics worked and her voice is back to normal. She offers to give him singing lessons as a thank you and together, they do a duet.

Kurt can't stand the fact that his dad has more in common with Finn and that the two of them keep going off to football matches together. He decides to bury the real him and become a mini-Burt instead: he dresses like his dad, sings 'Pink Houses' and makes out with Brittany. Burt catches Kurt and Brittany together and it really confuses him as he has spent years trying to accept that his son is gay. Despite Kurt's best efforts, his dad still spends time with Finn and his hurt son sings 'Rose's Turn' in the auditorium. Burt overhears Kurt and tells him that he loves him just the way he is; he doesn't want Kurt to pretend to be someone he's not.

In this episode Zack Weinstein guest-stars as Sean Fretthold. In real life, Zack is disabled and really wishes he had auditioned for Artie. Many Gleeks are hoping that Sean will reappear in Season 2.

This episode features covers of seven songs: 'The Lady Is a Tramp' by Sammy Davis, Jr, Miley Cyrus's 'The Climb', 'One' by U2, Rick Springfield's 'Jessie's Girl', 'The Boy Is Mine' by Brandy and Monica, John Mellencamp's 'Pink Houses' and 'Rose's Turn' from *Gypsy: A Musical Fable*.

Five of the songs were released for download and 'The Lady Is a Tramp', 'Rose's Turn' and 'One' were included on the soundtrack album, *Glee: The Music, Volume 3: Showstoppers*.

Lea Michele

Lea Michele is the super-talented actress who plays the lovely Rachel Berry in *Glee*. She was born in The Bronx, New York and grew up in Tenafly, New Jersey. Her ancestry is mixed: her mum is a Catholic-Italian-American and her dad is of Spanish-Sephardic Jewish descent. Lea is extremely close to her parents, who did everything they could to help their daughter become the actress she has always wanted to be.

Lea explained to Broadway Buzz: 'The one thing you will hear from anyone who ever worked with me – and I truly believe it's what helped me get so many jobs as a young kid – is that I have the coolest, most easy-going parents. Let me tell you, there were some crazy, crazy, crazy mothers out there. My parents would say, "This

SET SECRETS

Chris Colfer told Fox that not being able to laugh when Lea sings 'The Climb' badly was really hard and that during his kissing scene with Heather, he was told by the director that he was kissing too well, and that Kurt couldn't be a good kisser. It was actually the first onscreen kiss Chris had ever done, so he must have been quite nervous.

LEA MICHELE
LOOKING STUNNING.

[audition] is not a big deal," whereas other parents would look at their children and say, "You need to get this job."'

Michele has been busy acting for most of her life and made her debut on Broadway at the tender age of eight. She was accepted at the prestigious Tisch School of the Arts at New York University, but so far hasn't had time to go because she has been so busy acting on stage and now on TV, too.

At some point in their careers most actresses dream of being in *Les Misérables*, but Lea achieved this before her ninth birthday. She played Young Cosette and thoroughly enjoyed every minute on stage.

Lea revealed how she got into acting during an interview with talk show host Jimmy Kimmel. She told him: 'I auditioned for my first Broadway show when I was eight. A friend of mine was auditioning and I was just like, "Oh I'll go for fun just to... I don't know – I was jealous that she was going to do it, so I went as well and then I got it.'

Her friend ended up giving up her acting dreams and is now a successful writer.

Lea continued her education, but acted at the same time and so she must have shown quite a lot of dedication to be able to do both well. She would have had to do homework around performances and probably spent her holidays getting up to speed with the rest of her classmates.

Since her debut in *Les Misérables*, Lea has been in several big productions on Broadway including *Fiddler on the Roof*, *Ragtime* and *Spring Awakening*. She was over the moon when she found out that she was going to be in *Spring Awakening*: 'It was a pretty big deal. I think when we opened on Broadway I was about twenty, but I started working on it when I was really young, I did all the workshops and stuff like that. It was a pretty sort of intense role – I think that being on *Glee* now was a nice break from all that.'

In 2008, Lea returned to *Les Misérables* and this time played Eponine at the Hollywood Bowl. Her performance of 'On My Own' was outstanding and showed off her fantastic singing voice. She has also performed during the Tony Awards, which are the annual awards celebrating the best of Broadway and live theatre.

Despite being just in her early twenties and having a vast Broadway

LEA AND HER BEST FRIEND, CO-STAR JONATHAN GROFF.

résumé, Lea has also appeared in TV shows, too. She played Sammi in *Third Watch*, a drama about the lives of police officers, firefighters and paramedics in a fictional 55th Precinct and had a small part in the soap opera, *Guiding Light*.

As soon as Lea found out that a great new series called *Glee* was being made she knew that she wanted to be part of it. She told Backstage.com: 'The minute I read the script, already being a fan of Ryan Murphy, I was so excited to get the opportunity to audition. I immediately started fighting and making sure that I was able to get in. Like, every day I would call [my agent] and be like, "When am I going in for *Glee*? When am I going in for *Glee*? Make sure you stay on top of this project!" I really made sure that every day they were like, "When are you going to see Lea?"

'Being a singer and a performer, I really wanted to have the opportunity to be part of a show that I felt was tailor-made for my background. I had one audition, and then I went for studio and network. I found out later that Ryan Murphy – I had met him a year prior through a friend – had written the role for me so I kind of wish I would've known that before I went through all the nervous parts of auditioning [laughs].'

Even when Lea's agent got her an audition, it didn't go to plan. She was involved in a major car accident and had to leave her car where it was and walk to the audition, removing glass from her hair as she walked. Then when she finally arrived, things kept going wrong. She revealed to Thru.com: 'When I came into the room, the piano player completely messed up "On My Own." I stopped him in the middle and told him he needed to start it over. They were laughing at me and I told them to please stop laughing because this was a serious scene. Little did I know that all these little things were bits of Rachel Berry that were in me that I had no idea and then they were like, "That's perfect, it's great, come back" and in my head I'm like, "This is the worst audition of my life, I'm totally not going to get this," and I did.'

If you want to see Lea's audition for yourself, check it out on YouTube.

Glee creator Ryan Murphy has since explained to E! online: 'I knew Lea Michele because I did a pilot between *Nip/Tuck* and *Glee* called *Pretty/Handsome* about transsexuals, and that was with Jonathan Groff, who was in *Spring Awakening* in New York with Lea. So when I sold the *Glee* pilot and started to write down the part, I said there's only one girl who can play this. But no one would give her a deal because she had never done anything other than Broadway, so I told her, "I want you for this, but you're going to have to go through the whole cattle-call audition process," and she was just great. We never found anybody else, and then you do [the studio and network tests], and you're supposed to bring 10 people in, and I said she's the only one, and then she opened her mouth [and sang] and all the guys were crying, and they hired her, literally on the spot, in the room.'

It's great that he felt so passionate about Lea playing Rachel, even though she wasn't a big name. Now it's unimaginable to think that anyone else could play the part. Lea has such amazing onscreen chemistry with Cory Monteith, who plays Finn.

If you want to be an actor or actress, Lea has some auditioning tips for you. She confesses: 'I really don't like auditioning. I get so nervous; I'm so hard on myself. I sit at home and I'm like, "I'm not right for this, I'm not going to get it" – I come up with everything in my head – but I still go and I still do it, because this is what I love to do so. When it's over I'm like, so proud of myself so I guess I'd just say: just stick with it, go through it and then you know you'll be happy when it's over, that's how I feel.'

Lea likes to joke around and when asked by one interviewer what her approach to comedy was, she replied: 'My approach to comedy is just being me being funny. I find that I am a hilarious person so it's just really easy [laughs as she's joking]. No! Like we have the most incredible writers in Ian Brennan and Brad Falchuk and Ryan Murphy, they write the funniest stuff, and I go in and I'm like, "Okay, well I'm never going to be as funny as Jane Lynch, but I'm just going to go in and do my best today." And it's just great, it's just so fun – you know, being a part of a show that's a comedy but also at the same time has incredible dramatic moments; it just makes me so happy. I can come to work every day knowing that what I'm going to do is going to make me so happy and I try to honour the words these people have written for us.'

Before signing for *Glee*, Lea had never even heard of a Glee club and so she had no idea what they were. There was no Glee club in her school, but even if there had been then she probably wouldn't have been a member because she was so busy acting professionally on Broadway from a young age. She thinks it's great that fans of the show have been inspired to set up their own Glee clubs.

As with most of the *Glee* cast, Lea divides her time between her home in New York and Los Angeles, where *Glee* is filmed.

Like her *Glee* co-star Dianna Agron, Lea has a passion for animals and hates it when they are mistreated. She has joined with PETA (People for the Ethical Treatment of Animals) to protest against horse carriage riding in cities and says: 'As a New Yorker, I know how tough it can be to navigate the city streets, and that's on two feet! When I see the horses attached to carriages and made to pull heavy loads in traffic, it makes me sad and angry. I want tourists to know that long after their rides are up, these horses' miserable lives continue, day in and day out.'

LEA WITH *GLEE* CO-STAR
CORY MONTEITH.

M is for...

Mark Salling

Noah 'Puck' Puckerman on *Glee* is played by Mark Salling: he was born in Dallas, Texas, but moved to Hollywood as soon as he could to follow his dreams of becoming a star. He had to struggle to get where he is today as he had only his guitar and a suitcase when he first arrived.

Mark was determined to stay in Hollywood, no matter what, and made ends meet by working as a guitar tutor while studying at the Los Angeles Music Academy. His first love is music and he has been playing the guitar and piano since he was a child. He doesn't do covers and instead writes a lot of his own

MARK IS SUCH A CUTIE AND
LOVES TO SING.

music. One day, perhaps one of his tracks might be used in an episode of *Glee*.

His acting career started properly in 1996 when he played James Rhodes in the horror film *Children of the Corn IV: The Gathering*. Mark took one of the main parts alongside Naomi Watts and Karen Black. He was only fourteen when he shot the movie, but it was so violent and full of gore that it was given an 18 certificate when it came out on video.

His next big job was playing a character called Billy in one episode of *Walker, Texas Ranger*. He then went on to play Eric in *The Graveyard*, which was quite a big deal. His character fatally injures himself in a graveyard and years later the friends he was with at the time are murdered, one by one. It's definitely not a movie for the fainthearted!

Under the pseudonym of 'Jericho', Mark released an album in 2008 called *Smoke Signals*. His good friends Ryan Utterback, Ashley Johnson and Jay Logan all feature on it. The album is great and well worth checking out. Mark's fans will love the tracks: 'This Time of Year', 'Creature' and 'Wanderful' in particular. You can get the latest news on Mark's music and purchase tracks by visiting his website: www.marksallingmusic.com.

As well as creating great original songs to perform with his friends, Mark also writes for other musicians.

Danielle McKee and Josh Green have all used tracks penned by Mark.

Many people are under the impression that Mark, Lea and the rest of the *Glee* cast only had to do one audition to be cast, but it wasn't that simple. Mark had to audition five times before he was told that he had the part of Puck. It must have been so hard, going back in the audition room again and again, not knowing if they liked his interpretation of the character. Mark also had to prove that he could dance, which was a massive challenge for him – he had never really danced much before. He had to pull out all the stops and show everyone that he could act, sing and dance to win the part.

Because of his Mohawk hairstyle, Mark has to deal with a lot of interviewers jumping to the conclusion that he is a bad boy; they fail to recognise that he is just an actor playing a part. Sometimes he plays along with them and says he's even worse than Puck.

Part of Mark must wish that he could shave off the Mohawk and just have his regular haircut. He told one fan: 'I'm so over the Mohawk! I hate the Mohawk right now. It's okay, I'll keep it – I've just had it for so long. I've had it for like a year: I'm kind of over it, I'll feel better when I don't have it.'

Mark loves playing Puck and being one of the *Glee* cast. He is having the time of his life and enjoys hanging out with his new friends. Recently he posted a video on YouTube to thank Fox for picking him and to thank his cast mates for being so great. It shows him driving around Los Angeles singing into camera a song he has written. The lyrics are really moving. He talks of the fun they have each day and how everyone who works on the show is like family to him. The chorus is all about how there is nowhere he'd rather be than on set with his friends and the fact that they're going to be friends forever.

To date, Mark's favourite musical number has been 'Proud Mary' during the episode 'Wheels'. He told The TV Chick: 'It was great. We got to cruise around on little wheelchair ramps on stage and rehearsals for that one were a lot of fun.'

He doesn't mind that Puck has gone a bit soft to show Quinn that he could look after her and the baby, but he hopes that he'll get to go back to being bad soon. He liked throwing Slushies at people and attacking them with a Paintball gun. Bad guys are always far more interesting characters to play, and Mark and the rest of the cast can't wait to see what happens in Season 2.

If Mark was given the opportunity to pick any song to perform on *Glee*, then he would choose a song by Radiohead or rock band, Alice in Chains. His perfect guest star would be Nine Inch Nails' Trent Reznor because they might get the opportunity to perform some of his songs, like 'Closer', 'The Hand That Feeds' and 'Hurt'.

When The TV Chick asked Mark if he planned to release a solo album, he replied: 'I'm going to continue to write and record. I don't know how it's going to be released or anything, I'm just going to continue to be an artist and be creative, and hopefully I'll have an avenue to get it out.'

Mark might play a tough guy onscreen, but he is a real romantic at heart. He knows how to make a girl feel special and he confessed to one interviewer: 'In high school I had a girlfriend, and there was this field near where I lived. And I took her there, and I took rocks, and arranged them in a heart under a tree. And I didn't tell her – I just took her out there and walked her out and sat down, and was like, "Hey, look where we are!"'

'Mash-Up' – Season 1, Episode 8

The eighth episode of *Glee* was called 'Mash-Up'. It premièred in the USA on 21 October 2009 and first hit the UK screens on 22 February 2010.

In this episode Will is asked by football coach Ken and school guidance counsellor Emma if he will do a mash-up song for their rapidly approaching wedding day. Although he says that he will, he has a hard task ahead of him as the songs they have picked couldn't be more different: Sisqo's 'Thong Song' and 'I Could Have Danced All Night' from *My Fair Lady*.

Quinn and Finn begin to see that not everyone in the school is going to support them like their friends in the Glee club and they have Slushies thrown in their faces by other popular students. For the first time ever, they are becoming unpopular because their former friends don't want to be associated with them now that Quinn is pregnant and they are both in the Glee club. They are so upset that they go to visit Emma, but the only advice she can give them is to start wearing sunglasses because sunglasses are so cool.

In the music room Will sings 'Bust A Move' because none of the boys want to perform the song. But he shows them how it's done and they all start to join in.

Will and Emma have their first dance practice together, but it doesn't go too well. Emma is wearing a horrible eighties-style wedding dress and as Will performs the 'Thong Song', he trips on her train and they end up on top of one another. They don't know it, but Ken is watching and sees what happens. Even though Emma has said she will marry him, Ken knows that he is her second choice and that she would much rather be with Will, if he was available.

Ken decides to take it out on the Glee club by making sure that his football practice is at the same time as Glee club rehearsals so that Finn, Puck and the other guys who are in both the football team and New Directions can't show up for Will.

Rachel and Puck get close during a rehearsal at her house. Puck wants to make his mum happy by dating a Jewish girl and Rachel is eager for a distraction from Finn. When Rachel says she wants a man who isn't afraid to perform a solo, Puck takes it to heart and next time the opportunity arises, he performs 'Sweet Caroline' in front of the whole Glee club. As he serenades Rachel, Finn looks unhappy and Quinn starts to reconsider her decision to have nothing to do with Puck.

In this episode we also get to see a softer side to Sue as she falls head over heels in love with WOHN News 8 co-anchor Rod Remington. Being in love completely changes Sue's mindset: she decides to let bygones be bygones and stop her vendetta against Will. Sadly the good Sue isn't around for long and once she finds out that Rod is a love rat, she is back to her old ways and chucks Quinn out of the Cheerios because she doesn't want a pregnant cheerleader on the team.

Also in this episode, Will goes wedding dress shopping with Emma and Finn has a heart-to-heart with football coach Ken, who decides to change the times of his practices so they don't clash with the Glee club rehearsals.

The guest star in this episode was *Seven Pounds* actress Gina Hecht, who plays Puck's mother.

This episode featured covers of five songs 'Bust A Move' by Young MC, 'What a Girl Wants' by Christina Aguilera, 'Thong Song' by Sisqo, 'Sweet Caroline' by Neil Diamond and 'I Could Have Danced All Night' from the musical *My Fair Lady*. An instrumental version of the Louis Prima classic 'Sing, Sing, Sing' was used in the scene where Will teaches Sue how to swing dance.

SET SECRET

Puck nearly wasn't allowed to sing 'Sweet Caroline' for Rachel because Neil Diamond wasn't too keen on his song being used. He ended up retracting his clearance after they had filmed the scene and so the show's music supervisor P.J. Bloom personally went to Neil and was somehow able to persuade him to change his mind and give them the thumbs-up.

Shortly after 'Mash-Up' was shown on TV, Neil Diamond let his Twitter followers know that he enjoyed the performance by tweeting: 'Hey, so who's this guy Puck singing "Sweet Caroline" so good, so good, so good on #Glee? Loved it!!'

Neil Diamond wasn't the only one to like the *Glee* version of his song. When it was released for download alongside 'Bust A Move' and 'Thong Song', it did exceptionally well. It came in at number 34 in the USA, number 22 in Canada and number 37 on the Australian music chart.

'Sweet Caroline' and 'Bust A Move' were also picked for inclusion on the first *Glee* soundtrack – *Glee: The Music, Volume 1*.

INSIDER GOSSIP

The actors had to practise throwing the Slushie several times outside using a dummy so that they could get it right and it would hit Finn right in the face.

Cory says it was weird scraping the Slushie off his face and that he 'found it hard not eating this stuff.'

When Rachel gets hit in the face in 'Showmance' they used real ice-cold Slushies, but for 'Mash-Up' they made their own and so it was warmer. Chris Colfer also experienced the authentic Slushie and says it was much more painful because it was so cold – 'Like an iceberg!'

Matthew Morrison

The super-talented actor who gets to play Glee club director Will Schuester is Matthew Morrison. He is one of the most experienced members of the *Glee* cast and has studied at the prestigious Tisch School of the Arts in New York. His first big role was playing the gorgeous

MATTHEW IS SUCH
AN AMAZING SINGER.

Link Larkin in the 2002 Broadway production of *Hairspray* and he went on to star in many other big productions on Broadway.

Matthew was even nominated for a Tony Award for Featured Actor – Musical for his role as Fabrizio Nacarelli in *The Light in the Piazza*. It was an amazing achievement just to be nominated as the Tony Awards recognise the best on Broadway and in regional theatre. He was also nominated for a Drama Desk award for his performance in the Broadway musical *10 Million Miles*. The last Broadway show he did before being cast in *Glee* was *South Pacific* at the Lincoln Center Theater in New York.

As well as having lots of Broadway experience, Matthew has done lots of TV and film work too. He has appeared in *As the World Turns*, *CSI: Miami*, *Numb3rs*, *Law & Order: Criminal Intent*, *Ghost Whisperer* and many more TV shows. His film work includes the Steve Carell movie, *Dan in Real Life*, Chris Rock's *I Think I Love My Wife* and the Hugh Grant and Drew Barrymore flick, *Music and Lyrics*.

Unlike Cory Monteith who plays Finn, Matthew had a great time at school when he was growing up and so working on a series set in a high school brought up only positive memories.

Matthew told *TVGuide* magazine what it was like to be in high school for the second time around: 'I'm definitely getting paid more to go to high school this time around. I actually had a great experience at high school. I was kind of like that guy prom king, senior class president, star of like musicals, dating the homecoming queens.'

He divulged to another interviewer: 'I'm probably the only actor on our show who really enjoyed high school. I got the most out of it. I was really involved in so many programs. I was really into athletics, and I kind of had to choose at one point between playing soccer – which was my sport – and being in the musicals.'

Matthew was thrilled when he was informed that he had secured the part of Will because he felt a real connection to the character. He told NPR: 'Obviously the singing and dancing make it really special and suited to what I do well. If I could've written a role for myself, this would've been it. It's the perfect transition from going from stage into television.'

Indeed, he actually used some of his high school teacher's personalities and behaviours to flesh out Will and turn him from a few notes on a page into a real person.

Like many of the actors involved in *Glee*, Matthew loves rehearsing and performing the musical numbers best. He has sung some weird and wonderful songs during the first season, so who knows what he might be asked to sing in Season 2? His version of Kanye West's

'Gold Digger' and Sisqo's 'Thong Song' certainly stand out from the rest of the musical numbers.

Matthew explained to KOSU radio: 'The best part of going to work is when we're actually shooting a musical scene. You can just see it in all the crew because they've been doing shows for so long but they've never done anything like this. So to go to work and get to hear performances, it really just makes the whole vibe on set so special and so unique.'

'Mattress' – Season 1, Episode 12

The twelfth episode of *Glee* was called 'Mattress'. It premièred in the USA on 2 December 2009 and first hit UK screens on 22 March 2010.

In this episode Sue continues with her crusade to ruin the Glee club and this time, she manages to persuade Principal Figgins not to have a photo of New Directions in the school yearbook. The reason she gives him for this is that other students will just deface the photo anyway as they have in previous years. When Will finds out, he is furious as the Glee club have every right to a photo in the yearbook, like any other club or team in school. He pays for some advertising space in the yearbook out of his own money so that at least two members of New Directions can have their photos included there.

Will lets the Glee club members themselves decide

FOX

MATTHEW WITH HIS ON-
SCREEN WIFE JESSALYN.

who will be their two representatives and Rachel is first to be chosen – not because she is the most popular, but because the other members don't want to be in the photo because they know their faces will be defaced by the other students. It is Rachel's idea to have Finn as the second representative, but he is far from keen and drops out when his football teammates start poking fun at him.

When Rachel goes to get her photo taken she sees a great opportunity for New Directions to make them cool and popular. The photographer tells her he is just about to shoot an advertisement for the local mattress store owned by his brother-in-law, Randy Cusperberg. Rachel manages to get over how great it would be if the Glee club were in the ad and he buys into it – signing them up on the spot!

As well as feeling stressed about the school yearbook, Will is also concerned that Ken has booked the same day as the Sectionals for his wedding to Emma just to cause trouble. He lets Emma know his suspicions, but she refuses to accept that Ken knows anything about their flirty behaviour and says it must stop and she will be marrying Ken that day, no matter what.

Things get worse for Will when he realises that his wife Terri has been playing him for a fool for months and isn't carrying his baby, after all. He finds out that instead of telling him that she's had a hysterical pregnancy, she decided instead to concoct a plan to adopt Quinn's baby. A hysterical pregnancy is a fake pregnancy were a woman's body starts showing signs that she is pregnant even though she isn't. Will's head is all over the place: he decides that he needs to go somewhere else to think and so he heads for the school and ends up spending the night there, curled up on one of the free mattresses New Directions were given for taking part in the mattress store ad.

Sue delights in informing Quinn that because the Glee club received free mattresses as payment for taking part in the ad they are no longer seen as amateur and won't be able to compete at Sectionals after all. Will is distraught and says he will return the mattresses, but Sue insists that he can't because one has already been used.

Just when it looks as if things really could be all over for New Directions, Quinn comes to the rescue. She tells Sue that if the Glee club are no longer amateur then neither are the Cheerios as they have often received gifts and perks for being in the cheerleading squad. In a bold move Quinn demands that New Directions are given one of the pages reserved for the Cheerios. Sue reluctantly agrees and offers Quinn the opportunity to be in the remaining Cheerios photos for the yearbook. Even though Quinn has wanted to be back in the Cheerios for so long, she realises that things

Lea Michele, Matthew Morrison and Chris Colfer hold their Screen Actors Guild Awards. *Glee* won for best comedy ensemble.

The older cast members of *Glee* get together: Matthew Morrison, Jane Lynch, Jayma Mays and Jessalyn Gilsig.

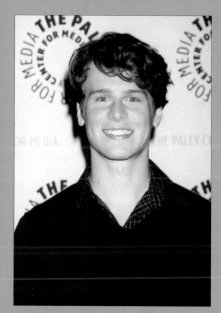

Glee relies on its amazing supporting actors to help give it a boost. *Clockwise from above left*: Jonathan Groff, Idina Menzel, Josh Sussman and Molly Shannon.

Above: The cast came out to watch the spring première of *Glee* with the fans at an outdoor screening.

Below: Heather, Mark, Kevin, Naya and Jenna get together for a night out.

Fans of *Glee*, more commonly known as 'Gleeks', show the love!

Playing the 'deliciously evil' Sue Sylvester has launched Jane Lynch into superstardom. She's the character everyone loves to hate!

Above: Jane out to lunch with her dogs and taking them for a walk.

Left: Jane can't go anywhere now without being followed around by the paparazzi.

Above: Some of the cast members muck around with a few of *Glee*'s producers. *Back row left to right*: Dante Di Loreto, Cory Monteith, Matthew Morrison, Outfest's Kristen Schaffer, Jane Lynch, Brad Falchuk. *Front Row*: Chris Colfer and Ian Brennan.

Below: The cast at a *Glee* première screening party.

Glee mania has officially taken over the world!

have now changed and she would rather be in New Directions any day.

Will really doesn't know whether he wants to be married to Terri anymore after all her lies and asks Emma what she thinks he should do. Rather than telling Will to dump Terri and ride off into the sunset with her instead, Emma decides to tell Will that she understands why Terri behaved as she did.

The Glee club have their yearbook photo taken and are excited about Sectionals, even though Will has stated that he won't be going because he was the one who accepted the mattresses and so they can't compete legitimately with him as their director.

The guest stars in this episode were *The Big Bang Theory*'s John Ross Bowie, who plays photographer Dennis, and *Poker Run*'s Chuck Spitler, who is the mattress store owner, Randy Cusperberg.

This episode features the *Glee* cast singing covers of four songs: 'Smile' by Lily Allen, 'When You're Smiling' by Louis Armstrong, 'Jump' by Van Halen and 'Smile' by Charlie Chaplin. The two 'Smile' songs and 'Jump' were released for download and appear on *Glee: The Music, Volume 2*.

SET SECRETS

The whole cast loved shooting the 'Jump' musical number on the giant mattresses. Chris Colfer admits: 'When we read the script and we found out that we were gonna be jumping on mattresses and trampolines we were like, "They're *paying* us to do this?" It was a dream come true for me!'

In fact, they all did really well to keep going because it was extremely hot in the warehouse where they were filming. Cory Monteith estimates that it was about 40°C (104F). Everyone had little fans to try and cool themselves down between takes so they wouldn't overheat. As he was fanning himself Chris Colfer jokingly said they were losing weight because they were sweating so much. Kevin McHale loved being in his blue PJs and found working on set with loads of mattresses made him feel really sleepy!

Filming wasn't all plain sailing, though. Dianna Agron (who plays Quinn) accidentally kicked Chris Colfer in the private parts and he also hurt his neck in a later take. Poor Chris!

Matt Rutherford (Played By Dijon Talton)

Matt Rutherford is a member of the football team and New Directions. He has a great singing voice and can dance too, but kept his skills a secret until recently as he wants to stay in the cool gang. After performing Beyoncé's

DIJON TALTON PLAYS
MATT RUTHERFORD

'Single Ladies' with the rest of the football team, he decided to join the Glee club alongside teammates Finn, Puck and Mike.

Dijon Talton who plays Matt feels that being in New Directions is encouraging the real Matt to come out. He explained to *Starry Constellation Magazine*: 'Slowly, but surely, I think he's getting more comfortable with "You know what, I'm going to be me, I'm going to be Matt Rutherford! I'm going to sing, I'm going to dance, I'm going to wear cowboy hats, and I am going to play football. It's okay to be more than a Lima loser forever!" I think he's finding himself, and what he really wants to do and what he really wants to be. He was the quarterback in football – he's not the Rachel Berry of *Glee*. He's finding himself and he's like, "You know what, at some point I think I'm ready to shine." I think he's just kind of feeling it out first.'

Though Matt might be considered more of a footballer than a performer by Rachel, Mercedes and Kurt, he picks New Directions over football practice when coach Ken makes him choose between the two in the 'Mash-Up' episode.

Mercedes Jones (Played By Amber Riley)

Mercedes Jones is one of the most outspoken members of New Directions. She has one of the strongest voices

AMBER RILEY PLAYS
MERCEDES JONES.

and refuses sometimes to accept what Will says. Rachel Berry might be seen as the lead female, but Mercedes is right up there too.

Her first performance of Aretha Franklin's 'Respect' proves that she can handle any song with ease. Mercedes is very close to Kurt and has a bit of a crush on him until she finds out that he is gay. They both love fashion and always try to look good, but still have to dodge the odd Slushie like everyone else.

Mercedes will always stick up for her friends and fans of the show love her for this.

Mike Chang (Played By Harry Shum Jr.)

Mike Chang is another member of the football team who joins New Directions after their 'Push It' performance. When Sue divides the group in half to try and cause trouble, she labels Mike the 'Other Asian'. The name sticks and he starts being called 'Other Asian' far more than Mike.

In Season 1, Mike is very much in the background, but Harry Shum Jr. who plays him insists that we will soon learn more about him once the other characters like Lea, Quinn and Finn have their storylines developed more.

MIKE CHANG IS
PLAYED BY
HARRY SHUM JR.

Music

Glee wouldn't be anything without the music: it holds each episode together and causes audiences to say 'Wow!' Each musical number is planned and structured as if it's a real performance – unlike the cast of the *High School Musical* movies, the cast don't break into spontaneous singing.

THE *GLEE* CAST LOVES TO SING!

Ryan Murphy is the man in charge of picking the songs for each episode and because he is one of the creators of the series and cares so much for it, he will go to any lengths to make sure that the songs he picks are the right ones.

Ryan wants *Glee* to appeal to everyone – he doesn't want to alienate people by choosing music from one genre or one decade alone and prefers to choose modern songs, old classics and Broadway numbers to create the perfect blend. He explained to the *Los Angeles Times*: 'I spend hours and hours listening to songs and picking songs that I like, or that I think will be great. I want there to be something for everybody in every episode. That's a tricky mix, but that's very important – the balancing of that.'

He also makes sure that each piece of music adds something to the episode it features in and fits in with the specific themes displayed in that episode too. Sometimes he dreams big and picks songs that he would love the *Glee* cast to perform, even though he doesn't think that the record labels will allow them to use the material. Quite often he is surprised when he gets the green light and some record labels are now suggesting songs that Ryan might use.

He talked about his passion for music to journalist Cristina Kinon: 'I was obsessed with *Grease* as a kid, I was obsessed with Journey, I was obsessed with Aretha

Franklin, so when we wrote the pilot, we wrote those songs in. Then in the process of getting them cleared, we were shocked that after a lot of these big artists and their companies read the script, they approved it.

'I think the key to it is they loved the tone of it. They loved that this show was about optimism and young kids, for the most part, reinterpreting their classics for a new audience.'

Lea Michele thinks that Ryan is really special. She told Billboard.com: 'Ryan Murphy's brain is iTunes. I've never met anyone with a music vocabulary as incredible as his. In the 13th episode, I go from singing a Barbra Streisand song into a Rolling Stones' song, into a Kelly Clarkson song.'

Ryan and the rest of the *Glee* creators decided to pick the best songs from each episode and put them on special *Glee* soundtracks, which have proved a huge success worldwide. The first album, *Glee: The Music, Volume 1*, charted at number 1 in the UK, number 3 in Australia and number 4 in the USA. Then the second album, *Glee: The Music, Volume 2*, charted at number 1 in New Zealand, number 3 in the USA and number 5 in Canada. In April 2010, the third *Glee* album was released, but this time all the tracks were Madonna covers. It was called *Glee: The Music – The Power of Madonna*.

Some singers are so keen for Lea, Cory and the rest

of the cast to sing their songs that they wave their licensing rates or offer them at reduced rates. When Ryan suggested that he might use original pieces of music in one episode he got a big response from people in the music business. As he explained to one journalist: 'I've had a lot of calls from songwriters, to the point where it's kind of embarrassing and ridiculous. So we're writing an episode called "Original Song", where the teacher asks the kids to write their own piece of music. Diane Warren is going to do two big ballads, and if it works, we'll see what happens but we won't do it all the time.'

As well as the *Glee* soundtracks we might soon be seeing other *Glee* albums, from the individual actors and actresses. They all have great potential and many of them can't wait to record their first solo album.

Ryan is excited about the prospect of buying Lea Michele and Amber Riley's albums in the future. He told Billboard.com: 'Lea has tried different songs and already thought, "Maybe I like doing rock." Her album is not going to be Broadway stuff – she'll sit with producers and come up with her own concept.

'I have no idea [who is bringing out an album], but all I know is that as soon as Amber Riley makes her album, I'm going to be the first one buying it!'

It will be so exciting for Amber if she gets to walk into a music store and see her album on the shelves.

After being rejected from *American Idol* all those years ago, it will be a huge achievement for Amber and her whole family.

N is for...

Naya Rivera

The super-talented actress who plays Cheerio and Glee club member Santana Lopez is Naya Rivera. A Los Angeles girl through and through, Naya is half-Puerto Rican, one-quarter African-American and one-quarter German. She got her first job when she was only a few months old: modelling and appearing in TV ads for K-Mart, an American discount department chainstore. Then, a few years later when she was four years old, she landed her first acting job. It was playing a character called Hillary Winston in Eddie Murphy's TV series, *The Royal Family*.

Naya was really in demand and appeared in several

THE BEAUTIFUL NAYA RIVERA IS
ALSO REALLY CARING.

other TV shows after *The Royal Family*. She had small roles in *The Fresh Prince of Bel-Air*, *Family Matters*, *Live Shot*, and *Baywatch* all before her eleventh birthday; she then went on to win roles in *Smart Guy*, *House Blend*, *Even Stevens*, *The Master of Disguise* and *8 Simple Rules*. Naya did so well to get these parts as she would have been up against seventy or more other children in each audition. She must have been gutsy to keep going to audition after audition while still studying at school. Naya admits that she is quite competitive, so this may well have played a part too.

In 2002, Naya secured a part in one episode of the hugely popular comedy, *The Bernie Mac Show*. She did so well that they invited her back to play Donna in another five episodes over the next four years. Things went a bit quieter for Naya after this, but she did get to appear in one episode of *CSI: Miami* in 2008.

Getting the part of Santana Lopez in *Glee* must have been a dream come true for Naya as it was the first time she had secured a major role in something with the potential to last for a few series if people liked it. It also allowed her to combine her passion for acting with singing. She had started writing her own songs when she was at school and has always had a passion for singing. In the future she would love to release a solo album.

She told journalist Angela Lee: 'I would love to launch a singing career because it's my greatest release and makes me feel the happiest. I'm currently writing new songs and taking my time with it because I really want it to be right if it happens. I'm still in the process of figuring out what style of music I'd like to do because I don't want to be like everyone else, so that's a bit difficult, but hopefully everything will fall into place and I'll be fortunate enough to make a good album!'

Before being cast in *Glee*, Naya had been thinking about putting her acting career on ice and trying something new. She had considered being a screenwriter instead, but luckily for us, she didn't quit the acting; she is a great actress and New Directions wouldn't have had quite the same buzz without her playing Santana.

Her motivation for wanting to try out for *Glee* was the opportunity to work with Ryan Murphy as she loved his previous series *Nip/Tuck* and was also keen to be in something different to the norm.

Glee fans are constantly saying that Naya is dating Mark Salling, but both deny that they are anything more than friends.

To play Santana, Naya thought about the mean girls that she met through school and based her character on them. People often think that Naya must have been Miss Popular at school because she is beautiful, but this wasn't the case: Naya didn't have lots of friends and was more interested in becoming an actress and so she joined clubs that would help her express her creative side.

You know you're a big star when your birthday party gets its own poster, like Naya's!

When she was asked by *Portrait* magazine what the vibe is like on the *Glee* set when they film the musical numbers, she replied: 'It definitely is both fun and challenging at times to put together all of the musical numbers. The good thing is that everyone has such a good attitude when it comes to the work that it makes it seem effortless. I love days when we shoot fast-paced musical numbers because everyone is running off adrenaline and working so hard that it's really rewarding. Typically for each number we will have a few days of rehearsal with our choreographer Zach Woodlee – who is amazing and just the best to be around – and then we'll shoot it. Sometimes it takes a lot out of you, but you get so much back at the end of the day.'

If Naya was in charge of picking the music for one episode of *Glee* you could expect a few tracks by Radiohead, The Ting Tings and USA singer Robin Thicke. She might enjoy working with Chris Colfer and Dianna Agron, but in an ideal world she would love to the opportunity to work with Johnny Depp and Kate Hudson too. Naya is really ambitious and would also seize the chance to do a bit of comedy on the sketch and variety show, *Saturday Night Live*. *Glee* fans would love to see her show off her amazing impressions on TV – she can do a great Jessica Simpson and Britney Spears!

Naya might have been acting since she was four years

old and be in one of the biggest TV shows of the moment, but she is determined not to let fame go to her head. As she explained to *Portrait* magazine: 'What keeps me grounded is the fact that I know just how tough the industry is. I think since I've been doing it for so long I've been up and I've been so down that it keeps everything in perspective for me. I know what it's like to book jobs and I know what it's like to have everyone say no for years at a time. I try to keep the mindset that even though I'm working right now on a popular new show, it's just that: I'm just working. It's what I love to do and despite all the perks and the praise at the end of the day, I'm just doing a job like everyone else. I happen to love the job, but it's just a job. I really try not to get caught up in the aspects of the industry and just be grateful that I get to feel productive every day.'

She also shared some advice for budding actors and actresses: 'I would say just keep pushing. I know it's really typical to say that you're going to have a million doors slammed in your face, but it really is difficult. You have to know that if you're committed to making it happen, it will happen. Always try, no matter how mundane it may seem, and know that there's a time for you.'

O is for...

Oscars

Lea Michele, Matthew Morrison and the rest of the *Glee* cast never thought for one minute that they'd be going to the Oscars so they must have felt like pinching themselves as they walked down the red carpet on 7 March 2010. They all looked so amazing as they posed for photos at Elton John's AIDS Foundation Academy Award Party, which took place after the main event and where they mingled with huge stars such as Miley Cyrus, Victoria Beckham, Hayden Panettiere and Jamie Foxx.

Harry Shum Jr. ('the other Asian') helped choreograph a dance routine for the Legion of Extraordinary Dancers

(LXD), who performed during the ceremony. He told Zap2It: 'I was so surprised and excited. You know, there are only so many seats. It's gonna be awesome. I'm in the process of getting my tux right now – I wanna make sure I look legit!'

P is for...

Patrick Gallagher

Patrick Gallagher is a Canadian actor of Chinese and Irish descent. He plays William McKinley High School football coach Ken Tanaka and is one of the oldest members of the *Glee* cast.

Patrick grew up in the Canadian city of Chilliwack, but once he decided that he wanted to become a professional actor he moved to Toronto and Montreal to attend theatre school there. He wasn't the most popular guy in school and struggled to know where he fitted in. The young Ken was a punk rocker and had a Mohawk; he also used a bit of black eye make-up to give him the 'right look.'

PATRICK GALLAGHER HOLDS
UP THE 'L' FOR LOSER SIGN.

Patrick is a very experienced actor and has had several big roles in TV shows and in movies. Usually actors are best known for playing one particular part, but he is best known for playing five characters: Detective Joe Finn in murder series *Da Vinci's Inquest*, Leon in police drama series *The Line*, Ken Tanaka in *Glee*, Awkward Davies in the Russell Crowe movie *Master and Commander: The Far Side of the World* and Gary the bartender in the comedy-drama movie, *Sideways*.

Patrick has appeared in over 60 more TV series and movies, including *Night at the Museum*, *Smallville*, *Final Destination 3*, *Stargate Atlantis* and *True Blood*. In the next two years he has several other big movies coming out, including *Legend of the Dancing Ninja* with David Hasselhoff.

His character might not yet have sung in *Glee*, but if the opportunity arose then Patrick would like to perform 'Creep' by Radiohead. He told the *Vancouver Sun*: 'I'm going to try and campaign hard for it. I did a rap this season, but I didn't sing for them. Sue Sylvester – who is played by the amazing Jane Lynch – and I are not really the singing ones, but we're all hoping to sing at some point.'

Ken might seem a bit of an oddball to us, but Patrick really likes his character. He explained to journalist Francois Marchand: 'I'm more like him than I care to admit. I realized I was going for what I like to think as an older version of me from years ago. I think Ken is not happy with where he is in life. I think he's still got a good heart, but there's this insecurity and bitterness piled on top of it.

'I think love is in Ken's head, and love for me is kind of an idealistic concept. But one thing I really respect about him is that he goes after something – he just doggedly pursues Emma. I wish I was more like that. In some ways, he's a little bit braver than I am. I mean, look at what he wears – that takes guts!'

In many ways the outfit that Patrick puts on to play Ken is really important. Jane Lynch also finds herself getting into character as soon as she puts on her trademark tracksuits.

Patrick really enjoys being on the *Glee* cast and likes the messages it sends out to teens. He thinks it shows that people are either bullied or are bullies themselves. He revealed: 'High school is tough but you know that the bullies deep down want to be in choir or in drama class. I think that's the message of this show that I really like: "It's OK to be different."'

'Pilot'

The first episode of *Glee* was simply called the '*Glee* Pilot' and was first broadcast in the USA on 19 May 2009. A few months later, on 2 September, the director's cut of the Pilot was broadcast a week before the second episode was shown so that those who missed it the first time around could catch up and those who had seen it then could have a refresh before the series started properly. The pilot didn't hit the UK screens until the middle of December 2009.

Because this was the first episode a lot of time was spent introducing the characters and the ideas that would be developed if *Glee* got the green light. In America, things work differently to the UK because pilots are made before full series are commissioned. This is to save money: if audiences don't like the concept of the show, then it is pointless to throw millions of dollars at it.

In this episode we meet Spanish teacher Will Schuester for the first time and see him replace Sandy Ryerson as director of the William McKinley High School's Glee club after Sandy is fired by Principal Figgins for inappropriate behaviour towards a student. Will wants to return the Glee club to its former glory dating back to when he was a student. He decides the Glee club needs a fresh start and renames it New Directions.

After Will holds auditions for places in the Glee club he finds the first five members of New Directions: overconfident Rachel Berry, loud and brash Mercedes Jones, disabled musician Artie Abrams, stuttering Tina Cohen-Chang and the camp Kurt Hummel.

Rachel might be the most talented member of the Glee

club, but she tells Will that she's going to quit unless he can find a male vocalist who can sing and dance as well as she can. She doesn't like the fact that Will currently has Artie as the lead male singer because his wheelchair restricts what they can do and she is sick of being made a laughing stock.

After Will has another meeting with Principal Figgins he is told that he can't use the auditorium for Glee club practices because the Principal wants to hire it out to paying groups. Eventually, they come to a compromise: New Directions can use the auditorium until Nationals and if they prove that they are one of the best Glee clubs around, then they can continue to use it. If they bomb at Nationals, however, then they lose their rehearsal space.

Will bumps into the former Glee club director when he's out shopping and Sandy tells him that he's happy not to be working as a teacher any more – he's making a fortune re-selling medical marijuana to other teachers. Will can't believe what he's hearing and is really shocked when Sandy slips him a packet for free.

Knowing that he needs more quality performers to join New Directions, Will approaches cheerleading coach Sue Sylvester, but she says that none of her girls would ever consider being in the Glee club because they are the most popular kids in school whereas the Glee kids are right at the bottom of the food chain. He then turns to the football team in the hope that a few of them might join.

After getting permission from the school's football coach, Ken Tanaka, Will puts up an audition sheet for the football jocks to sign up to, if they are interested in joining New Directions. But no one takes it seriously and only made-up names appear on the list. Then Will walks past the changing rooms and hears Finn singing in the shower.

Will realises that Finn is the talented singer that he is looking for and that he could be the only person who can encourage Rachel Berry not to quit. He decides that the only way to persuade Finn to join New Directions is by pretending that he found the packet of marijuana that Sandy gave him in Finn's locker and so he blackmails him into joining the Glee club. It works because Finn doesn't want to let his mum down and secretly, he knows that she will be delighted that he is performing.

Will wants to inspire New Directions and takes them to see another Glee club – Vocal Adrenaline – perform. Emma Pillsbury, the school's guidance officer, tags along too as she has a bit of a crush on Will. Vocal Adrenaline's performance of Amy Winehouse's 'Rehab' goes down a storm, which worries Rachel, Mercedes and the rest of New Directions because they don't know whether they'll ever be good enough to compete against other Glee clubs like that.

As soon as Will gets home, Terri breaks the news that they are expecting their first child. Providing for his family becomes Will's priority: he knows he needs to get a better job than teaching. He tells the members of New Directions that he will be leaving school in two weeks as he has applied to become an accountant.

Finn's football mates can't believe that he has joined the Glee club and rip into him. This makes him want to leave New Directions but when he sees the football team trap Artie in the portable toilet so they can tip it over, he realises he is different. He apologises to his new Glee friends and they all decide to stick together to make it to the Nationals: he's going to be in the football team *and* in New Directions. As they practise 'Don't Stop Believin'', Emma asks Will to take up the role of Glee club director again and he realises that he has to – he would hate it if they won without him.

The *Glee* pilot was a massive success. It was viewed by 9.619 million viewers when shown for the first time on 19 May and was the fourth most-viewed show on the Fox network for that week. Another 4.2 million saw the director's cut in the September. Straight away fan sites were set up and favourable reviews appeared in newspapers and magazines. The night it aired for the first time, it was the top topic on Twitter. Journalist Mary McNamara wrote in her review for the *LA Times* that *Glee* was: 'the first show in a long time that's just plain full-throttle, no-guilty-pleasure-rationalizations-necessary fun.' *Entertainment Weekly*'s Ken Tucker loved it too and said in his review: 'Has there ever been a TV show more aptly named than *Glee*? It both embodies and inspires exactly that quality.'

There were 10 songs covered in the *Glee* Pilot. The cast sang 'Where is Love?' from *Oliver!*, 'Respect' by Aretha Franklin, 'Mister Cellophane' from *Chicago*, 'On My Own' from *Les Misérables*, 'Sit Down, You're Rockin' the Boat' from *Guys and Dolls*, 'You're the One That I Want' from *Grease*, 'I Kissed a Girl' by Katy Perry, 'Can't Fight This Feeling' by REO Speedwagon, 'Rehab' by Amy Winehouse and 'Don't Stop Believin'' and 'Lovin', Touchin', Squeezin'' by Journey.

The director's cut version of the *Glee* Pilot also included an acoustic version of 'Leaving on a Jet Plane' by John Denver.

Four of the songs covered by the *Glee* cast were released for download. The songs chosen were 'On My Own', 'Can't Fight This Feeling,' 'Rehab' and 'Don't Stop Believin''. All four songs were big hits worldwide, especially 'Don't Stop Believin''. It charted at number 2 in the UK, number 4 in the USA and Ireland, number 5 in Australia, number 16 in New Zealand and number 50 in Canada. What's more, it was also number 1 in the USA iTunes chart after more 302,000 people downloaded it after seeing the pilot. Wow!

People loved the *Glee* Pilot so much that it was nominated for three Teen Choice Awards. It was in the Choice TV: Breakout series category, Cory Monteith (Finn) was nominated for Choice TV: Breakout Star Male and Lea Michele (Rachel) was nominated for Choice TV: Breakout Star Female. They were up against *90210*, *Fringe*, *J.O.N.A.S!* and *The Secret Life of the American Teenager* in the Breakout series category. Cory was up against Frankie Jonas, Daren Kagasoff, Danny McBride and Tristan Wilds for Breakout Star Male, while Lea had Demi Lovato, AnnaLynne McCord, Chelsea Staub and Anna Tory in the same category for Breakout Star Female.

They might not have ended up winning any of the awards but it was a fantastic achievement just to be nominated. Later in 2010, they will no doubt clean up with lots of Teen Choice Awards as fans will have watched a whole season of *Glee* by then. In years to come, they will no doubt win countless Teen Choice Awards.

'The Power of Madonna' – Season 1, Episode 15

The fifteenth episode of *Glee* is called 'The Power of Madonna': it premièred in the USA on 20 April 2010 and first hit the UK screens on 26 April 2010.

In this episode Sue wants the Cheerios to take a

leaf out of Madonna's book and has Principal Figgins play some classic tracks from the diva over the school intercom.

Rachel, Mercedes and Tina sit and discuss how boys make them feel. Rachel talks about the pressure she feels to have sex and Tina admits that Artie wants her to wear more revealing clothes. Will overhears them and wonders if he can do anything to help.

Will goes to one of Sue's cheerleading training sessions

MADONNA AND HER DAUGHTER, LOURDES, BOTH LOVE *GLEE*.

and sees the Cheerios perform to Madonna's 'Ray of Light'. This makes him want to set a Madonna theme for New Directions, but Sue isn't happy that he's stolen her idea. Kurt and the girls are so excited, but Puck and the boys don't want to sing Madonna songs.

Kurt and Mercedes feel sorry for Sue when Will insults her and so they give her a *Vogue*-style makeover. Emma, Rachel and Finn tell their partners (or in Finn's case, Santana) that they are ready to lose their virginity. Emma and Rachel end up backing out at the last minute, but Finn does sleep with Santana. Later he lies about it to Rachel.

Jesse announces that he has transferred to William McKinley High and from now on, he will be a member of New Directions. Rachel is over the moon that she can date Jesse without any resentment from the others but fails to realise that they still think he's a spy, who will steal solos from the boys, too. Mercedes and Kurt in particular are upset that Jesse will be in New Directions and so they make up their minds to join the Cheerios. After the boys perform 'What It Feels Like for a Girl' they decide that they need to change the way they treat the girls and Artie apologises to Tina for what he said about her needing to wear more revealing clothes. Finn tells Rachel that he won't try and come between her and Jesse.

Madonna has granted *Glee* the rights to her entire

catalogue of music, though understandably, not for free.

In this episode the cast performed eight Madonna covers: 'Like A Virgin', 'Vogue', '4 Minutes', 'What it Feels Like for a Girl', 'Express Yourself', plus a mash-up of 'Borderline' and 'Open Your Heart' and 'Like a Prayer'. A new album containing all the songs was released – *Glee: The Music – The Power of Madonna* – and it reached number one on the Billboard 200.

Madonna herself told *US Weekly* magazine, 'I thought the Madonna episode of *Glee* was brilliant on every level. The dialogue and the entire script was genius. I completely appreciated the layers of irony, especially when all those macho boys sang 'What it Feels Like for a Girl'.

Madonna had watched the show with her kids before it aired on television and said, 'I also loved the fantastic performances of "Vogue", "Express Yourself" and all the messages about the boys being respectful to girls ... The entire cast was amazing. They're all so talented. I especially loved Sue Sylvester and Kurt Hummel's characters. Ryan Murphy did a great job bringing all these elements together. Lola loved the show too. I wish I went to a high school like that ... if only!'

'Preggers' – Season 1, Episode 4

The fourth episode of *Glee* was called 'Preggers'. It premièred in the USA on 23 September 2009 and first hit the UK screens on 25 January 2010.

In this particular episode Kurt is caught by his dad dancing to Beyoncé Knowles' 'Single Ladies' with Brittany and Tina. Rather than admit that it is a dance routine (and have his dad think he might be gay), Kurt decides to lie and tells him that it is football exercise and that he has joined the team. His dad is so chuffed and says he wants to see his son play.

Kurt doesn't want to disappoint his father and so he persuades Finn to help him get onto the football team. Finn tells his coach Ken that Kurt can kick and he agrees to let him try out. Despite mocking from the rest of the football team, Kurt takes a kick after doing his Beyoncé dance and gets it right on target. Ken is excited about having such a great kicker on the team.

When Finn finds out from Quinn that he is going to be a dad, he is gobsmacked: he didn't think she could get pregnant because they haven't actually slept together, but he takes her at her word that it happened when they were in the hot tub. Knowing that Quinn is expecting makes Finn wonder what the future holds: he wants to win a football scholarship, but knows this will never happen unless his team start winning games. He asks Will to teach the football team to dance because he thinks this will give them the edge; he also confides in his best friend Puck that Quinn is expecting his baby, not knowing that Puck is the real daddy.

Terri gets caught out by her sister, who realises that she isn't expecting Will's baby but has had a hysterical pregnancy instead. Instead of telling Terri that she must let Will know the truth, she simply smiles and says they will just have to get her a baby. When Terri finds out that Quinn is expecting, she decides to offer her some advice and suggests that she gives her the baby for adoption.

Meanwhile, nothing is off-limits for Sue when it comes to ruining the Glee club and she decides to have the disgraced Sandy reinstated so that he can help her bring down Will and his students. She blackmails Principal Figgins into letting Sandy back into the school as the new Arts director by saying that if he doesn't agree, then she will put up an embarrassing video of him on YouTube. As soon as she gets her way, she sets about arranging auditions for the new school musical in the hope that Rachel Berry will ditch the Glee club for the starring role.

Sue gets her wish as Rachel quits the Gee club when Will gives the lead solo part to Tina for a change and won't back down when Rachel objects.

Also in this episode, Kurt teaches his new football pals how to dance to 'Single Ladies' and after initially saying that they won't perform it in the actual game because they are concerned that they will be mocked by their peers, they decide in the final seconds that they should. With their opponents stunned into silence, they launch an attack and thanks to Kurt, they achieve the vital touchdown.

Afterwards, Kurt is so happy as he goes through his nightly beauty regime that he decides the time is right to tell his dad that he is gay. His father informs him that he has known ever since he was a little boy and loves him just the same.

This episode contains less covers than other episodes as the Beyoncé Knowles' 'Single Ladies (Put a Ring on It)' dance routine was performed several times. The cast also sang 'Taking Chances' by Céline Dion and 'Tonight' from the musical *West Side Story*. 'Taking Chances' was also released for download and appears on the first *Glee* album.

The guest star in this episode was experienced character actor Kurt Fuller, who plays the local news station owner, Mr McClung. Kurt has appeared in *Wayne's World*, *Ghostbusters II*, *Ugly Betty*, *Desperate Housewives* and numerous other TV shows and movies. More recently, he played the angel Zachariah in *Supernatural*.

Principal Figgins (Played By Iqbal Theba)

Principal Figgins is the man who is supposed to be in

INSIDER GOSSIP

When Chris Colfer first found out that he would be performing Beyoncé Knowles' 'Single Ladies' in 'Preggers' he panicked because he didn't know if his limited dancing skills would be up to it.

Actually, there was no need to worry because Chris was given three choreographers to help him and he had five weeks to rehearse and learn it. It's a complicated number but Chris was able to make it look relatively easy by the time the cameras started to roll.

The black outfit he wears when performing 'Single Ladies' with Brittany and Tina is something that Chris himself came up with because he didn't want to end up wearing a Beyoncé-style leotard with big heels. He admits that might have caused him to need years of therapy!

charge of William McKinley High School, but he is prone to getting things wrong. For a time, Sue Sylvester manages to blackmail him and he is forever cutting budgets.

Glee fans love Principal Figgins for three reasons: he has a cool accent, makes great videos and cuts the Cheerios' budget so New Directions can have some costumes. They dislike him when he lets Sue have her own way and fails to back up Will.

Promotion

Part of the reason why *Glee* has been a big hit from day one is because of the way that the cast has promoted the show. They all care so much about the series that they wanted to make sure that as many people as possible were watching it.

They held episode premières, went on a promotional tour of the USA and sang 'The Star-Spangled Banner' at the third game of the 2009 World Series. This baseball match is huge and over 15 million watched their performance on TV. Wow! It definitely made people sit up and take notice, and wonder just who were the kids from *Glee*.

The cast had planned to have a float at the 2009 Macy's Thanksgiving Day Parade in New York, but they were told that they couldn't do this after TV broadcaster NBC objected as they were hosting the parade and *Glee*

THE KIDS OF *GLEE* WENT OUT ON A 'GLEEK' TOUR THAT WAS REALLY POPULAR.

would be airing on a rival station. Both the show's creators and cast were disappointed by the decision and Ryan Murphy quipped to EW.com: 'I completely understand NBC's position, and look forward to seeing a Jay Leno float.'

For Christmas 2009 the cast recorded their own version of Wham!'s 'Last Christmas', which didn't appear in an episode but was released for download. It charted at number 46 in Canada, number 60 in Australia and number 63 in the USA .

Since *Glee* has become the biggest show on the box it has been announced that there will be a tour so that the fans can get up close and personal with their favourite actors and actresses. Lea, Cory, Amber and co. will perform the best musical numbers and the audience will be able to sing along, too. Sadly for UK *Glee* fans there are no plans for international concerts just yet, so they will have to make a trip to the USA if they want to enjoy the '*Glee* Live in Concert' tour.

Other shows have been keen to get a bit of the *Glee* magic too. *The Family Guy* spin-off, *The Cleveland Show*, decided to feature an animated Rachel, Finn, Kurt and Will in one of their episodes. Lea Michele was ecstatic and according to TV Guide said: 'It was awesome to do. I'm a huge *Cleveland Show* fan and I've been literally stalking them to let me come on!'

Chris Colfer added: 'All Kurt says is "Marc Jacobs" and "Broadway" because that's all Kurt knows.'

Puck (Played By Mark Salling)

Noah 'Puck' Puckerman is the bad boy of William McKinley High School. He is a bully and generally thinks that he is better than everyone else. It's a bit surprising that he is Finn's best friend because Finn is so nice and caring – the complete opposite of Puck.

When Finn first joins New Directions, Puck is gobsmacked because cool guys don't join Glee clubs. But when he finds out that Quinn is carrying his baby, he changes his mind and joins the Glee club to spend time with her. Because his mum wants him to go out with a good Jewish girl, he starts to date Rachel but they split once he realises that she only went out with him to make Finn jealous.

MARK SALLING, WHO PLAYS PUCK, WITH HIS SIGNATURE MOHAWK HAIRSTYLE.

Q is for...

Quinn Fabray (Played By Dianna Agron)

When Season 1 starts, Quinn Fabray is one of the most popular girls at William McKinley High School as she is the captain of the cheerleading squad and is dating the captain of the football team, Finn Hudson. However, her world is turned upside down when she realises that she is pregnant with Finn's best friend's baby. Instead of telling Finn the truth, she tells him he's the daddy, even though they have never actually had sex. She also considers giving the baby to Terri, the pushy wife of Will Schuester.

Quinn joins the Glee club under the instruction of Sue Sylvester because the Cheerios coach badly needs them to

QUINN FABRAY WITH HER BABY-DADDY, PUCK.

fail. She becomes Sue's spy and reports back everything that happens; she also helps to stir up trouble whenever she can, with the help of her cheerleader pals, Brittany and Santana.

As time progresses, Quinn's loyalty is divided as she is thrown off the cheerleading squad once Sue discovers that she is pregnant and the other popular kids in the school give her a hard time. Her friends in New Directions vow to support her throughout her pregnancy and will do anything to make her smile again.

R is for...

Rachel Berry (Played By Lea Michele)

Rachel Berry is the most talented singer in New Directions – and she knows it. She signs her name with a gold star at the end because she thinks that one day she'll be a big star. Rachel is really focused about what she wants to do and won't let anything get in the way of her singing ambitions; she hates it when Will gives solos that she wants to do to other people and even quit the Glee club in protest when Will gave Tina the solo 'Tonight' from *West Side Story*. She joins the school musical instead but soon realises that she has made a big mistake.

Like all the founding members of New Directions she

RACHEL BERRY WITH HER
ON-AGAIN, OFF-AGAIN BOYFRIEND
JESSE ST. JAMES.

isn't very popular and gets Slushies thrown in her face by the football team. The Cheerios also enjoy taunting her whenever they can. Even the other members of New Directions find Rachel highly annoying, but they can't dismiss the fact that she is super-talented.

Rachel's life revolves around musicals, singing and Finn. She has a huge crush on Finn and they do kiss, but nothing more happens because Finn is dating Quinn and they wrongly think that she is carrying his baby. Puck might be a jock, but he starts to date Rachel, only for them both to admit they have feelings for someone else. Rachel can't get Finn out of her head and Puck wants Quinn to choose him over Finn.

Ryan Murphy

Ryan Murphy is a hugely successful writer and producer. He is one of the three guys who created and developed *Glee* into the fantastic show we see on television. Ryan is best known for creating the plastic surgery drama, *Nip/Tuck*, and the teen comedy-drama, *Popular*.

Born in Indianapolis, Indiana, Ryan was an only child. At school, he was always excitable and admitted that he was gay when he was fifteen. He loved performing from a young age and was in a choir. When he was at Indiana University, Bloomington he was interested in becoming a journalist so he worked on the college paper. On graduating, he worked for the *Miami Herald*, the *Los Angeles Times*, *New York Daily News*, *Knoxville News Sentinel* and *Entertainment Weekly*.

In the late 1990s Ryan started to write screenplays and was lucky enough to have Steven Spielberg buy his script: *Why Can't I Be Audrey Hepburn?* Sadly it has never been produced, but it could well be in the future.

A few years later he made the move into television with his teen-comedy, *Popular*. It ran for two seasons, from 1999 to 2001. He then went on to do the Golden Globe winning *Nip/Tuck*, which premièred on 23 July 2003 and ran for six seasons. The show concluded on 3 March 2010.

As well as writing for *Nip/Tuck*, Ryan continued

Right to left: Dante Di Loreto, Brad Falchuk, Ryan Murphy and Ian Brennan.

writing screenplays. In 2006, he wrote and directed *Running with Scissors*, a great film starring Alec Baldwin and Annette Bening. It was based on a memoir by Augusten Burroughs and was nominated for a Golden Globe.

Ryan also did a couple of pilots, but they didn't get taken up. The networks didn't feel that the sitcom *St. Sass* and the transsexual comedy *Pretty/Handsome* warranted being made into full series. He must have been thrilled when the *Glee* pilot got the thumbs-up in 2009.

Ryan might be busy with *Glee*, but he is still directing and writing screenplays. In the next two years he has some great movies coming out, such as the comedy *Dirty Tricks*, starring Sharon Stone, Meryl Streep and Jim Broadbent, *Eat/Pray/Love* with Julia Roberts, and *Alfred Hitchcock and the Making of Psycho*, starring Anthony Hopkins.

Working on something as fun and groundbreaking as *Glee* has been a dream come true for Ryan Murphy, Ian Brennan and Brad Falchuk. It is a very different show than anything the creators have ever done in the past.

Journalist Brian Gianelli from Fancast.com asked Ryan if there had been any pressure from Fox to dumb the show down. He replied: 'Actually, I've always been hesitant to do a network show. I've never had much luck with it just because I think my voice is pretty specific and a little bit subversive. And I told Kevin Reilly when I pitched it that if I was going to do it, I wanted to do it in a very specific way, and Kevin was the person who bought *Nip/Tuck* in the room, so he kind of got my sensibility.

'And to my surprise and utter pleasure, Fox has really kept their word. In fact, they're pushing me to make it much more in the vein of the pilot, and they've never once tried to take anything out because they thought it was too sort of nuts, but I've also been very conscious that I think the key to the show is to – it's a show with a lot of heart, and it's a show about underdogs, and you want it to have a certain kindness to it. But it also does have weird elements, but they've been very supportive of those, knowing that that's my tone, and that's what keeps me interested, so I've been surprised, and it's been a really great give-and-take so far.

'But also, I want to do a show that appeals to everybody. I've done a cable show and that to me was a big challenge. I've done sort of eight years of darkness and really adult stuff, and I was like, OK, I want to try something different. I want to do a show that has a bigger heart and is kinder, but make no mistake: it still has an edge, and they've been supportive of that.'

Even before Season 1 of *Glee* aired Ryan and the other

creators had offers from people wanting to turn *Glee* into a Broadway show and an ice-skating extravaganza. Everyone knew it was going to be a big success and they wanted to be part of it.

S is for...

Sandy Ryerson (Played By Stephen Tobolowsky)

Sandy isn't one of the most popular *Glee* characters by a long way. He was the director of the Glee club until he was fired for inappropriate behaviour. When he bumps into Will out shopping, he reveals the he's been selling medical marijuana. Sue blackmails Principal Figgins into letting Sandy back into school so he can be in charge of Will and the creative arts side. She wants to bring New Directions down and she knows that getting Sandy on board will help.

Sandy is a creepy guy, who is obsessed with Josh Groban and collects music boxes and dolls.

Santana Lopez (Played By Naya Rivera)

Santana Lopez might be beautiful, but her personality isn't: she always makes sure that she puts herself first and isn't afraid to upset people. She loves boys, especially Puck, and is a stereotypical cheerleader.

Santana is one of the Cheerios who joins the Glee club and initially helps Sue by trying to cause friction between the members of New Directions. She might be friends with Quinn, but when her boyfriend Puck goes babysitting with Quinn, she decides that she needs to warn Quinn off. She isn't prepared to let Quinn snatch her man and tells her that Puck was sending her sexy texts the night before.

In the episode 'Sectionals', however, Santana admits that she likes being a member of New Directions and says that it's the highlight of her day.

Schedule

The *Glee* cast's schedule is pretty jam-packed the whole time. At the beginning they had more time to prepare and practise, but now they have to shoot, rehearse, shoot... there's no time to waste!

It's much more demanding being an actor or actress on *Glee* rather than on other shows. They are so busy that they hardly have any time to sit back and relax with their feet up. Even when they're not filming, they are taken all over the world to promote the series. They

NAYA RIVERA,
WHO PLAYS
SANTANA LOPEZ.

found being in Australia particularly strange as many of the cast had never been that far away from home before. Chris Colfer told one Australian interviewer: 'Its my first time away from the United States, ever.'

Shelby Corcoran (played by Idina Menzel)

New Directions' biggest competitor Vocal Adrenaline is coached by Shelby Corcoran. She is Rachel Berry's birth mother, but hadn't seen her daughter since she was a baby until Sectionals. Shelby persuades Jesse to move schools and get close to Rachel, so he can encourage Rachel to want to meet her birth mother. Jesse plays Rachel a tape of Shelby singing and Rachel recognises Shelby by her voice when she sneaks into a Vocal Adrenaline rehearsal. Also in Season 1, Shelby makes out with Will and offers him relationship advice. At Sectionals, she rejects Rachel's request to help coach New Directions and instead adopts Quinn's baby, Beth.

'Showmance' – Season 1, Episode 2

The second episode of *Glee* was called 'Showmance'. It was shown in public for the first time at Comic-Con in July 2009, but actually premièred on television in the USA, two months later, on 9 September 2009, and first hit the UK screens on 11 January 2010.

In this particular episode Will is on a quest to find

some new members for the Glee club as they need at least 12 more people to compete at Nationals. He thinks the best way for them to impress the other students with their musical abilities is if they perform during a school assembly. According to Will, the Chic song 'Le Freak' would be perfect, but Rachel, Mercedes, Artie and the rest of the New Directions are less than impressed. Will listens to them and ditches the song for Kanye West's 'Gold Digger' as a compromise.

Rachel will do anything if it means spending time with Finn and so joins the celibacy club, even though his girlfriend Quinn goes, too. Quinn really can't stand Rachel at all and encourages her friends in the club to pick on her.

Rachel is still not happy with Will's song choice and thinks they can do better but instead of raising her concerns with him again, she goes behind his back instead. She tells the other members of New Directions that they should sing 'Push It' by Salt N Pepa, which they do, much to Will's horror.

This musical number causes Will a big headache as angry parents complain to Principal Figgins about the inappropriate lyrics. He then decides that Will must only choose songs from a list he has written himself – which restricts Will's creativity enormously.

Even though what Rachel did was wrong, their performance of 'Push It' did encourage the other students to think that being in the Glee club wouldn't be quite so uncool as they had originally thought and Will soon has a keen Quinn, Bethany and Santana asking him if they can join New Directions. He knows that having three cheerleaders who can sing and dance will be a great asset to the club and help them do well at Sectionals.

Will decides to teach Rachel a lesson and gives Quinn her solo on 'Don't Stop Believin''. He might think that Quinn has honest intentions for joining the Glee club, but her loyalty will always lie with the Cheerios. Sue persuades her to act as her eyes and ears, and to help make other members of the Glee team question Will's ability to be their director.

Things are never easy for Will and his home life is just as complicated as his work. His wife Terri insists that they will need a bigger house when the baby comes, so he ends up getting an extra job to do in the evenings. He becomes one of the school's janitors and gets close to Emma during a shift. Football coach Ken notices their flirty behaviour and tells Emma to watch that she doesn't become a 'rebound girl'. Emma takes what Ken says onboard and when Will wants to spend time with her, she tells him she can't because she's going on a date with Ken instead.

Also in this episode, Terri finds out that she is having a hysterical pregnancy so there will be no baby. Instead of telling Will the truth, she decides to say that she has found out the sex of their baby and they are going to have a son. Rachel and Finn rehearse together and end up sharing a kiss, but Finn has an 'accident' and tells Rachel that it's Quinn that he wants to be with, not her.

In this episode Valorie Hubbard guest starred as Peggy. Valorie is an experienced Broadway, television and movie actress, and also teaches others how to act in Los Angeles. She has most recently been in *True Blood*, *How I Met Your Mother* and *Hannah Montana: The Movie*.

The *Glee* cast do covers of five songs in this episode. They perform 'Take A Bow' by Rihanna, 'Push It' by Salt N Pepa, 'Gold Digger' by Kanye West, 'All By Myself' by Eric Carmen and 'Le Freak' by Chic.

Three of the covers were released for download: 'Gold Digger', 'Push It' and 'Take A Bow'. Lea Michele's version of 'Take A Bow' was a big hit with *Glee* fans worldwide. It nearly didn't happen, though, as *Glee* creator Ryan Murphy explained to Alex Strachan from the Canwest News Service: 'We wrote an episode around Rihanna's "Take a Bow", which I thought we would never, ever get the rights to. Because, usually, people who have No.1 hits, even if they give it to you, want hundreds of thousands of dollars, in my experience. But Rihanna gave it to us for a really good price.

'That's been one of the cool and surprising things about this experience, that these people that the cast and we really admire and respect have found out about the show and are supportive, to the extent that some of them have even come to us and said, "Here, use this for free." I got a CD only yesterday from a company that had, like, 25 songs – huge songs – that they are excited for us to do our version of. It's been quite remarkable.'

INSIDER GOSSIP

It was during rehearsals of Salt N Pepa's 'Push It' that the cast really bonded. Lea Michele explained at Comic-Con: 'It was so much fun to do. Reading the script, I didn't think we would be as "offensive" as it was, but we had a lot of fun filming it – a lot of fun!'

Stephen Tobolowsky

The actor who plays oddball Sandy Ryerson in *Glee* is Stephen Tobolowsky. Since 1976, Stephen has been acting professionally and has appeared in over 200 different TV shows and films. He has played doctors, principals, attorneys and even a caveman during his varied career. His most famous roles were playing Ned Ryerson in *Groundhog Day* and Bob Bishop in *Heroes*.

Stephen might be best known for his film and TV work, but he actually graduated from Southern Methodist University with a major in theatre. He went on to act in plays in Los Angeles, New York and San

Francisco, and also did a bit of directing too. Stephen was such a talented actor that he was nominated in 2002 for a Tony Award for Best Performance by a Featured Actor in a Play.

Sue Sylvester (Played By Jane Lynch)

Sue Sylvester is a character *Glee* fans love to hate. She is the coach of the Cheerios at William McKinley High and is determined that her girls will be the best cheerleaders around. Sue sees the Glee club as a threat to the future of her cheerleaders as she doesn't want to have to share the limelight (or budgets) with them.

She enlists Quinn, Santana and Brittany to join New Directions in an attempt to bring them down from the inside. To get more control, she blackmails Principal Figgins into making her the co-director of the Glee club and later leaks their set lists for Sectionals to their competitors. Sue will do whatever it takes to get her own way and wipe the smile from Will Schuester's face.

JANE LYNCH PLAYS
SUE SYLVESTER.

T is for...

Terri Schuester (Played By Jessalyn Gilsig)

Terri Schuester is the wife of Will Schuester and she'll do anything to keep her man. They might have been high-school sweethearts, but Terri knows she has to do something more to guarantee he sticks around. When she finds out that she's pregnant she's thrilled, only to discover later that she's experienced a hysterical pregnancy and is not having Will's baby after all. Rather than tell him the truth, she comes up with a plan to get cheerleader Quinn to hand over her baby.

Terri is so scared that Emma Pillsbury will steal Will away that she gets a job as the school nurse so she can keep an eye on her. She is also jealous of the Glee club

JESSALYN GILSIG
PLAYS TERRI
SCHUESTER.

THE

as she hates the fact that Will spends so much time with rehearsals and performances.

TVGuide.com asked Jessalyn Gilsig why her character lies to Will and if she is afraid to lose him. She replied: 'Oh yeah! In so many ways, she's still in high school. You know how in high school you have those ridiculously hair-brained plans, like if I wear his sweater home, he'll have to call me because I have his sweater? I think Terri still lives in that world, where I can move the pieces in such a way to create a picture, and that will make it real.

'She's married and she loves him. Their communication is really weak and she's missing a lot of the skills for the marriage. She has no desire to lose him and she certainly doesn't have the desire to lose him to a redhead with a bob. She's like, "Look at me, I'm a cheerleader, why would he go to the redhead?" She'll do whatever she thinks she has to do. I'm sure there might be a better way, but whatever she thinks is the best way to keep him home – the longer he's home, the greater the chance that he's going to stay there. That's as far as her intellect takes her.'

'Theatricality' – Season 1, Episode 20

The twentieth episode of *Glee* is 'Theatricality': it premièred in the USA on 25 May 2010 and first hit the UK screens on 31 May 2010.

In this episode Tina is told by Principal Figgins that she must stop dressing like a Goth. Will realises that the Principal actually believes vampires are going round the school. At first Tina does as she is told, but the other members of New Directions can't accept that she is now wearing clothes that don't express who she is. At the end of the episode, she is back in her usual attire: she approached Principal Figgins late one night in the corridor sporting fangs and told him that if he didn't let her wear what she wanted, then she'd send her Asian vampire father to bite him.

Also in this episode, Rachel sneaks into their rivals' auditorium and watches Vocal Adrenaline practising a Lady Gaga number for Regionals. She tells Will and he instructs New Directions to go Gaga and prepare their own Lady Gaga song. The girls and Kurt love the opportunity to create their own crazy costumes and perform a fantastic version of 'Bad Romance'. However, the other boys in Glee Club hate having to perform a Lady Gaga song and refused to do so, instead picking 'Shout It Out Loud' by Kiss.

Puck puts his foot in it again when he suggests to Quinn that 'Jackie Daniels' would be the perfect name for their daughter. She's not impressed and he goes away, determined to come up with a better name. Later in the rehearsal room he wants to prove that he is serious about being a father and sings 'Beth' – Quinn is impressed with his performance and tells him that he can be present when she gives birth.

While spying on Vocal Adrenaline, Rachel suddenly realises that Shelby is her mother. She walks over to Shelby's desk and introduces herself – she's so happy to have finally found her, but it feels weird at the same time. Later, Rachel calls on Shelby again to ask her to help her sew a better Lady Gaga costume – her dads cannot sew at all.

Will is pleased that Rachel has found her mother, but feels he must have a little chat with Shelby. During their heart-to-heart, Shelby confesses that she is unable to have any more children, but wishes she could have her baby back to look after her, rather than the teenage Rachel. Will says she must tell Rachel the truth.

Rachel and Shelby admit to each other how they are feeling and Shelby suggests that instead of trying to act like mother and daughter, they should just be grateful for one another but keep a bit of distance from each other for a while. They hug and before Shelby goes, Rachel asks her to sing with her.

Meanwhile, things aren't going too well in the Hummel household. While Kurt might be delighted that Finn and his mother are moving in with him and his dad, Finn can't think of anything worse. He hates the way Kurt decorates their room and in anger, he describes some of the things in it as being 'faggy'. Burt overhears and tells him that the word is unacceptable and he can no longer have Finn living in his house, even if it upsets Carole.

Back in school, Kurt has been threatened because of his Lady Gaga-inspired ensemble, but he tells the bullies that they'll just have to beat him up: he's not about to change who he is. Finn arrives in the nick of time and tells them to back off, all the while dressed in a red rubber outfit he's made from a shower curtain. It looks as if both Kurt and Finn are about to be beaten up, but the rest of New Directions appear and so the bullies are forced to flee.

In this episode the cast cover five songs: 'Poker Face' and 'Bad Romance' by Lady Gaga, 'Beth' and 'Shout It Out Loud' from Kiss and 'Funny Girl' from the movie of the same name. All five were released as singles, with 'Bad Romance' included on *Glee: The Music, Volume 3: Showstoppers*. 'Poker Face' and 'Beth' were included on the deluxe version of the album.

Chris Colfer told Fox that this episode was his favourite to date, for his character, Kurt Hummel.

'The Rhodes Not Taken' – Season 1, Episode 5

The fifth episode of *Glee* is titled 'The Rhodes Not Taken'. This episode premièred in the USA on 30

September 2009 and first hit the UK screens on 1 February 2010.

In this episode Will wonders how he can find a talented female singer to replace Rachel Berry as she has left New Directions for the school's musical instead. He needs to do something if his Glee club has any chance of doing well at Sectionals, which are rapidly approaching.

Will enlists the help of Emma to check past pupil records and finds out that the girl who was the star of the Glee club when he was at the school never actually graduated. He quickly forms a plan in his head and sets out to trace April Rhodes.

When he goes to meet April in her huge home he thinks that she has made an enormous success of her life but when an estate agent walks in, he realises that she doesn't own the house at all and that she has a huge problem with drink. Her life is going nowhere so, as they sit on a kerb with their feet in the dirt, Will challenges her to come back to school, join the Glee club and graduate.

April might be a great singer, but straight away she proves to be a bad influence. Poor Emma is distraught when she releases the methods that April has been using to get the Glee club singers to like her: she gets Kurt drunk to boost his confidence and teaches Tina and Mercedes how to be the perfect shoplifters. After Will finds out from Emma what is going on, he tells April that she must stop drinking. She agrees, but continues to drink in secret.

Finn is really confused about what the future holds for him now that he is about to become a dad and goes to see if school guidance counsellor Emma can offer him any advice. She suggests that if he wants a scholarship he should go for a musical one rather than a football one – and that getting Rachel back in New Directions would improve his chances enormously.

Finn decides to take Rachel bowling to make it look as if he's interested in her and to convince her to join the Glee club again so they can spend more time together. Rachel is already unhappy at how things are turning out with the school musical anyway – Sandy is constantly trying to pull her down by saying her singing is off – and so she quits so that she can return to the Glee club to be with Finn.

Rachel doesn't remain in New Directions for long, though, as she quits as soon as she finds out that Quinn is pregnant and realises that Finn only took her bowling to get her back in Glee club.

The Glee club's performance of 'Last Name' goes down a storm when they perform it in front of a full house and April is thrilled to get a standing ovation. During the interval she tells Will that she's leaving – school isn't for her and she needs to move on and do something else instead. This puts New Directions in a predicament as they still have to sing 'Somebody to Love' and now they don't have a lead female. Rachel steps in and manages to do an amazing job, even though she doesn't know the choreography.

The guest star in this episode was Kristin Chenoweth, who played April Rhodes. Kristin is best known for playing Annabeth Schott in *The West Wing* and Olive Snook in *Pushing Daisies*. She has had a successful Broadway career too and received a Tony Award for playing Sally Brown in the musical *You're a Good Man, Charlie Brown*. The Glee creators was thrilled when this experienced singer came on board.

Kristin told TV Guide: 'The cast is superb and the writing is dead-on. I truly had a blast playing this character! This part is like nothing I've had the chance to do on TV. She's very happy when drinking to ease her pain. I also sing in three very different styles, which is always fun and challenging.'

In this episode the *Glee* cast covered six songs: 'Don't Stop Believin'' by Journey, 'Last Name' by Carrie Underwood, 'Maybe This Time' and 'Cabaret' from *Cabaret*, 'Somebody to Love' by Queen and 'Alone' by Heart.

'Maybe This Time', 'Last Name' and 'Alone' were released for download. 'Somebody to Love' was the most popular, getting to number 28 in the USA and

number 33 in Canada. All three tracks were included on
Glee: The Music, Volume 1.

INSIDER GOSSIP

The first time Chris Colfer heard Kristin Chenoweth sing
'Somebody' he was so moved that he cried. When
they shot the scene for real, he decided to increase the
crying and have Kurt wipe his eyes with a tissue for
maximum effect.

Matthew Morrison loved the opportunity to work with Kristin
and thinks she's amazing. He admitted to the *Los Angeles
Times*: 'Kristin Chenoweth is kind of like a powerhouse in this
really short girl. She's kind of a genius, everything she does
is so, intricate, like she's so detailed in her comedy and it's
kind of amazing to watch.'

Cory Monteith added: 'She walked into the room and she
learnt the dance number that we'd been rehearsing for a few
days in fifteen minutes. She's so good at what she does, she's
the real deal. I learnt so much from watching someone with
that much talent just do their thing.'

'Throwdown' – Season 1, Episode 7

The seventh episode of *Glee* was called 'Throwdown'.
This episode premièred in the USA on 14 October 2009
and first hit UK screens on 15 February 2010.

In this particular episode Will is gobsmacked when Sue becomes co-director of New Directions and decides to split the group in two so they can each sing a song in Sectionals. She wants to cause as much trouble as possible, so handpicks all the 'minorities', leaving Will with just Rachel, Finn, Puck, Quinn and Brittany.

Will is so angry with Sue that he decides to fail all her cheerleaders, who are awful at Spanish, and this means they can't be cheerleaders because the school rules state that they need to pass all their subjects to be in the cheerleading squad.

Finn and Quinn attend their ultrasound appointment and find out that they are going to have a daughter. Will is thrilled for them both and tells Terri that he will be booking an ultrasound appointment ASAP for them because he wants to see their baby too. Terri panics, but after she visits the obstetrician with her sister Kendra she is able to use blackmail to fake the scan and fools Will into thinking that he is seeing their baby onscreen.

Finn tells Quinn that he has come up with the perfect name for their daughter 'Drizzle'. Quinn is less than impressed and tells a deflated Finn that she plans to have the baby adopted. Time is running out before the whole school gets to find out that its golden couple are having a baby as the school reporter and gossip king Jacob Ben

Israel is keen to spread the news. Only Rachel is able to temporarily stall him.

During practice, Sue and Will start arguing and screaming at each other. The members of New Directions walk out – they just can't stand what's happening. Sue and Will realise that their behaviour is wrong, Sue vows to step down and Will decides to pass her cheerleaders so that she can have them back in her cheerleading squad.

Sue finds out that Quinn is pregnant and makes Jacob run the story, even though she knows it will cause Quinn a lot of pain. Rachel, Mercedes and the rest of the Glee club members rally round Quinn and show her that they will stand by her, no matter what, by singing 'Keep Holding On' by Avril Lavigne.

The guest star in this episode was Amy Hill, who plays Dr. Chin. She is best known for playing Mrs. DePaulo in *That's So Raven* and Mrs. Kwan in Dr. Seuss's *The Cat in the Hat*.

This episode featured covers of five songs :'Ride Wit Me' by Nelly, 'Hate On Me' by Jill Scott, 'You Keep Me Hangin'' On' by The Supremes, 'No Air' by Jordin Sparks and 'Keep Holding On' by Avril Lavigne.

'No Air', 'Hate on Me', 'Keep Holding On' and 'You Keep Me Hangin'' On' were all available for download and are included in the first *Glee* album.

INSIDER GOSSIP

Jane Lynch's favourite scene was in the Principal's office when her character argues with Will and then he pokes her and leaves the room. She gets so angry that she goes to grab a student and Principal Figgins shouts, 'Not the children, Sue!' Jane, Matthew and Iqbal improvised most of the scene and did such a great job.

Tina Cohen-Chang (Played By Jenna Ushkowitz)

Tina Cohen-Chang is the shy Goth kid in New Directions. She loves being part of the group and having real friends. Because of the way she looks Tina gets picked on by the football team and members of the Cheerios.

Will recognises that Tina has a beautiful singing voice and he wants to help her to reach her full potential. He gives her a solo, which angers Rachel and causes her to leave the group.

After they share their first kiss, Tina admits to Artie that she has been pretending to have a stutter. He is furious because he can't believe someone would lie about something like that.

JENNA USHKOWITZ
PLAYS TINA
COHEN CHANG

Tour

When an actor signs up for a TV show they expect that it will be just that, a TV show and maybe a bit of publicity. For the members of the *Glee* cast, it was much more: they were to release albums and maybe have the opportunity to release their own original music too.

On 1 March 2010, it was announced that the *Glee* cast would be doing a tour of the USA, calling at Phoenix, Los Angeles, Chicago and New York. Rumours had been circulating that a *Glee* tour was on the cards for quite a while after Cory Monteith tweeted: 'This show has changed my life in so many ways. If you had told me a year ago that I'd be performing classic rock songs in concert theaters around the country, I would never have believed you. We are psyched!'

The official statement only confirmed what *Glee* fans already knew.

It might be just a small tour with seven dates, but '*Glee* Live! In Concert!' could go worldwide in future if there is enough demand. *Glee* fans everywhere would love the opportunity to hear 'Don't Stop Believin'', 'Somebody to Love' and 'Jump' sung live by their favourite actors and actresses.

Ryan Murphy told billboard.com: 'The response of the fans to our little show has been so immediate and so gratifying, we wanted to get out and thank them live and in person.'

U is for...

Ulrich, Robert J.

Robert J. Ulrich is one of the amazing casting directors who helped to find the perfect *Glee* cast. He is very good at what he does and has been the casting director for *Nip/Tuck*, *The Mentalist*, *Saving Grace* and lots of other top shows.

The Casting Society of America even gave Robert an Artios Award for Outstanding Achievement in Casting – Television Pilot – Comedy for *Glee*. It was his second award: the first Artios Award that he received was back in 2003 for Best Dramatic Episodic Casting for *Nip/Tuck*.

The other casting directors on *Glee* are Eric Dawson and Carol Kritzer.

Underdogs

Glee is a TV show about underdogs. It's not about the most popular kids in high school or even the most polished Glee club in America, it's about a group of underdogs who come together to create something that is truly inspirational.

Everyone who watches *Glee* can relate to at least one member of the Glee club, whether it is one of the geeks, a cheerleader or a jock. We're all underdogs at some point in our lives and *Glee* teaches people how to rise above this and succeed.

V is for...

'Vitamin D' – Season 1, Episode 6

The sixth episode of *Glee* was called 'Vitamin D'. This episode premièred in the USA on 7 October 2009 and first hit the UK screens on 8 February 2010.

In this episode Will decides to get the New Directions members working harder as Sectionals are rapidly approaching. He splits them into boys vs girls and sets them the task of coming up with the best mash-up.

Meanwhile, Sue continues her vendetta against Will and this time she gets dirty by trying to ruin his marriage. She approaches Will's wife Terri and warns her that the school's guidance counsellor Emma Pillsbury has feelings for her husband. This panics Terri and forces her to take action: she decides to get a job at the school so that she can keep an eye on Will and Emma. Even though she is not medically qualified, she somehow manages to become the school nurse. When football coach Ken drops by, she tells him that he needs to propose to Emma. Terri also corners Emma and warns her to stay away from Will. She gets some good news when Quinn pays her a visit and tells her that she can adopt her baby.

Finn finds playing for the football team and being the lead singer in the Glee club really tiring. He goes to visit Terri, who gives him some of her pseudoephedrine tablets. Pseudoephedrine is a decongestant which can help relieve nasal or sinus congestion (stuffiness). Instead of being tired, Finn has a newfound energy and quickly shares them with the rest of the boys so they can come up with an amazing performance to beat the girls, who believe they have already won. The girls don't even think they need to rehearse until they see Finn, Puck and the rest of the guys perform their mash-up of 'Confessions' and 'It's My Life'.

Rachel and the other girls find out from Kurt that the boys have taken tablets to give them energy and so they visit Terri to enhance their performance of 'Halo' and 'Walking On Sunshine'. Principal Figgins finds out and is so angry that he fires Terri and makes Sue the new co-director of the Glee club so that she can keep an eye on things.

The guest star in this episode was Joe Hursley, who

plays Joe. Joe is a talented actor and musician, but started out as a prankster on the TV series *You've Got a Friend* and *Punk'd*.

This episode featured two mash-ups containing two covers each, 'Halo' by Beyoncé Knowles and 'Walking On Sunshine' by Katrina & The Waves, 'It's My Life' by Bon Jovi and 'Confessions Part II' by Usher. Both mash-ups did exceptionally well when they were released for download. The boys' mash-up charted at number 14 in the UK, number 25 in Canada and number 30 in the USA. The girls' mash-up reached number 9 in the UK, number 28 in Canada and number 40 in America.

INSIDER GOSSIP

Lea Michele found the musical numbers a lot tougher in 'Vitamin D' compared to those in the other episodes because the singing and dancing had to be a lot faster and so the cast needed much more energy, too.

If Lea found it hard, Cory must have found it even more difficult – the boys' mash-up was a lot more intense because they were doing a rock'n'roll number. They had to be so angry, and run around doing high kicks, acting all crazy – they must have been so tired after every take!

W is for...

'Wheels' – Season 1, Episode 9

The ninth episode of *Glee* was called 'Wheels'. It premièred in the USA on 11 November 2009 and first hit the UK screens on 1 March 2010.

In this particular episode Will is told that the school can't afford to pay for a bus with disabled access to take New Directions to Sectionals, so Artie won't be able to travel with them. Will doesn't think this is right and suggests they raise the necessary cash by selling cakes to the other students. The other members of New Directions don't really understand why Artie just can't follow the bus in his parents' car. To teach them of the daily battles that Artie has to go through because he is confined to a wheelchair, Will gets each member of the Glee club a wheelchair and orders them to spend time in it.

Meanwhile, everything's not so rosy for poor Finn. He is getting grief from Quinn, who wants money to pay for her ultrasound, and even his best mate Puck is giving him a hard time because he thinks Finn is letting Quinn down.

Puck wants to ensure the cake sale is a big success and so he slips cannabis into the cakes. He tries to give all the money they make to Quinn, but she refuses to take it.

Back in the Glee club, both Kurt and Rachel want to sing 'Defying Gravity'. Rachel is the one given the nod, but after Kurt's dad tells the Principal that his son is being discriminated against, Kurt gets a chance to audition. He ends up doing a bad audition on purpose after his dad gets an abusive phonecall because 'Defying Gravity' was written for a female to sing – he doesn't want his dad to get any hassle.

It looks like New Directions will have a new couple when Artie and Tina kiss, but it all goes pear-shaped when Tina confesses that she has been lying for years about having a speech impediment. Artie is crushed and wonders whether he can carry on being in the Glee club.

Sue knows that she must find a replacement for

Quinn and after holding auditions, gives Becky Jackson the spare place. No one expected Sue to opt for a girl with Down's Syndrome and Will is astounded when Sue hands over her own cash to pay for three new handicap ramps for disabled pupils at the school. It seems she has a soft side after all as it's revealed that her own sister has Down's Syndrome and now lives in a residential home.

The guest stars in this episode were Cheryl Francis Harrington, who previously starred alongside Eddie Murphy in the 1999 comedy, *The PJs*, and Jeff Lewis, who recently played Vork in the award-winning online sitcom, *The Guild*. Both Cheryl and Jeff played nurses in this episode. This episode also introduces two recurring characters: Becky Jackson, played by Lauren Potter, and Jean Sylvester (Robin Trocki).

'Wheels' features the *Glee* cast singing covers of three songs: 'Defying Gravity' from the musical *Wicked*, 'Dancing With Myself' by Generation X and Tina Turner's version of the John Fogerty song 'Proud Mary'. All three tracks were released for download, with 'Defying Gravity' proving to be the most popular. It came in at number 31 in America and number 38 in Canada.

DID YOU KNOW...?

The battle Kurt goes through to be able to sing 'Defying Gravity' was actually based on what happened to Chris Colfer when he was at school. 'Defying Gravity' is his favourite song, but he was never allowed to sing it because he was a male – even though he kept asking and asking every year.

Glee creator Ryan Murphy explained to the *Los Angeles Times*: 'I told him, "Well, you came to the right show runner, mister!" And I found a way to write it into the show because that's in a nutshell what this show is about: someone being told that they can't do something because of what the perception of them is, as opposed to what their real ability is.'

Chris was over the moon to get the opportunity and told the paper in an email: '[It] really meant the world to me. It's absolutely terrifying to watch yourself do something you've dreamed about for such a long time. I know I'm definitely not the best singer, but I think the message, the story behind the song about defying limits and borders placed by others, hopefully all that gets across with the performance. Although I do some very "Kurtsy" things in the song, it's probably one of the most honest and close-to-heart scenes I've ever filmed or performed for that matter.'

White House

The cast of *Glee* was shocked when they learned that Michelle Obama had invited them to perform at the White House Easter Egg Roll on 5 April 2010. Cory Monteith thought it was 'poppycock'.

On the day itself Amber got to open with the National Anthem and then the whole *Glee* cast got to perform 'Somebody to Love', 'Somewhere Over the Rainbow', 'Sweet Caroline', 'True Colors', 'Home', and 'Don't Stop Believing'. It was an amazing experience and one the whole cast will remember forever.

Chris Colfer tweeted 'I feel like today was a dream! I met the President of the United States, JK Rowling, and Ellen's Mom Betty DeGeneres! so surreal!'

Jenna tweeted 'Sang at the White house, watched @msamberriley kill the national anthem on the WH balcony and met the OBAMAs!!!! What?!?!?! Best Day Ever.'

Will Schuester (Played By Matthew Morrison)

Will Schuester is the Spanish teacher at William McKinley High School and after the former director of Glee club is sacked, he takes over the role. He re-names the Glee club 'New Directions' and aims to make it as successful as it was when he was a member at the same school: he wants to take them to Nationals and see them win.

WILL SCHUESTER IS
PLAYED BY MATTHEW
MORRISON.

Will constantly comes up against cheerleading coach Sue Sylvester, who wants to ruin his plans, and he has to cope with the demanding student Rachel Berry on a daily basis, too. He is married to Terri, who was his high-school sweetheart, but their relationship isn't going too well. At first, Will is shocked when he finds out that he is to become a dad, but soon he can't wait to see his baby son for the first time. He has no idea that Terri isn't really pregnant and that she plans to take Quinn's baby. When he eventually finds out the truth, he leaves Terri and shares a kiss with guidance counsellor Emma Pillsbury, who has had a crush on him for a long time.

X is for...

XO Necklace

When Lea Michele decided to wear a gold 'XO' choker length necklace when filming 'Throwdown' and 'Mash-Up' she had no idea of the fuss this would cause. As soon as the episodes aired, fans of the show went on forums demanding to know where they could buy the 'Rachel Berry necklace'.

It was actually Lea's own necklace given to her by her mum, but that didn't stop fans from searching high and low for it. They were delighted to find out that it was available to buy for $403 and that its proper name was the 'Zoe Chicco Pave Hug & Kiss Necklace'. Rachel Berry fans have been buying their own 'XO' necklaces ever since.

Y is for...

YouTube

If you love *Glee*, then you must head over to YouTube as there are over 14,000 *Glee* videos on there. You can watch all the behind-the-scenes videos, see the cast audition for their parts and look at fab fan videos, too.

Some members of the cast have recorded special messages to *Glee* fans that are only available on YouTube, so be sure to check them out.

Z is for...

Zach Woodlee

The super-talented choreographer behind all the *Glee* musical numbers is Zach Woodlee. He has been the choreographer on lots of top films and TV shows, including *27 Dresses*, *Hairspray* and *Eli Stone*. Zach is also a talented dancer and has supported Madonna on her 'Re-Invention Tour', Mandy Moore on her tour and performed alongside LeAnn Rimes on several TV shows, too. He even appeared in a Pepsi ad with Britney Spears!

Zach manages to come up with five to eight fantastic routines for each episode of *Glee* and teaches the cast their routines in record time. Ryan Murphy might be the one who picks the songs and the cast may be the ones singing, but it is Zach who adds the magic with his routines. *Glee* is a very expensive TV show to produce as each episode takes up to 10 days to film because of Zach's choreography. It costs at least $3 million to make an episode.

Zach thinks the most talented dancer out of the *Glee* cast is Kevin McHale, who plays Artie. Although Kevin has to stay in his wheelchair during filming when the cameras aren't rolling he helps his friends learn their choreography when they are struggling to pick up the dance moves.

So far, the hardest musical number for Zach to choreograph has been 'Proud Mary' from the 'Wheels' episode, which saw every member of New Directions perform in a wheelchair. He explained to the *New York Post*: 'It was like roller derby. All of the actors would fall backwards and hit their heads – particularly Lea Michele, who plays Rachel. You lose your balance really quick when you try to go up a ramp in a wheelchair. Amber Riley, who plays Mercedes, caught an edge going down a ramp and fell off completely. There were pile-ups, there were crashes – basically, everything that could go wrong, did!'

SOME OF THE *GLEE* CAST MAKE THE DAY OF A FEW LUCKY FANS BY POSING FOR A PICTURE!